CW01333787

GARNISH

ELEVATE YOUR PLATE

Written by

Pia Warner

A publication of nosh publishing LLC. 2021.

To all of the people who will throw mint leaves on anything and call it a garnish, this is for you

A VISUAL GUIDE TO PLATING BEAUTIFUL FOOD

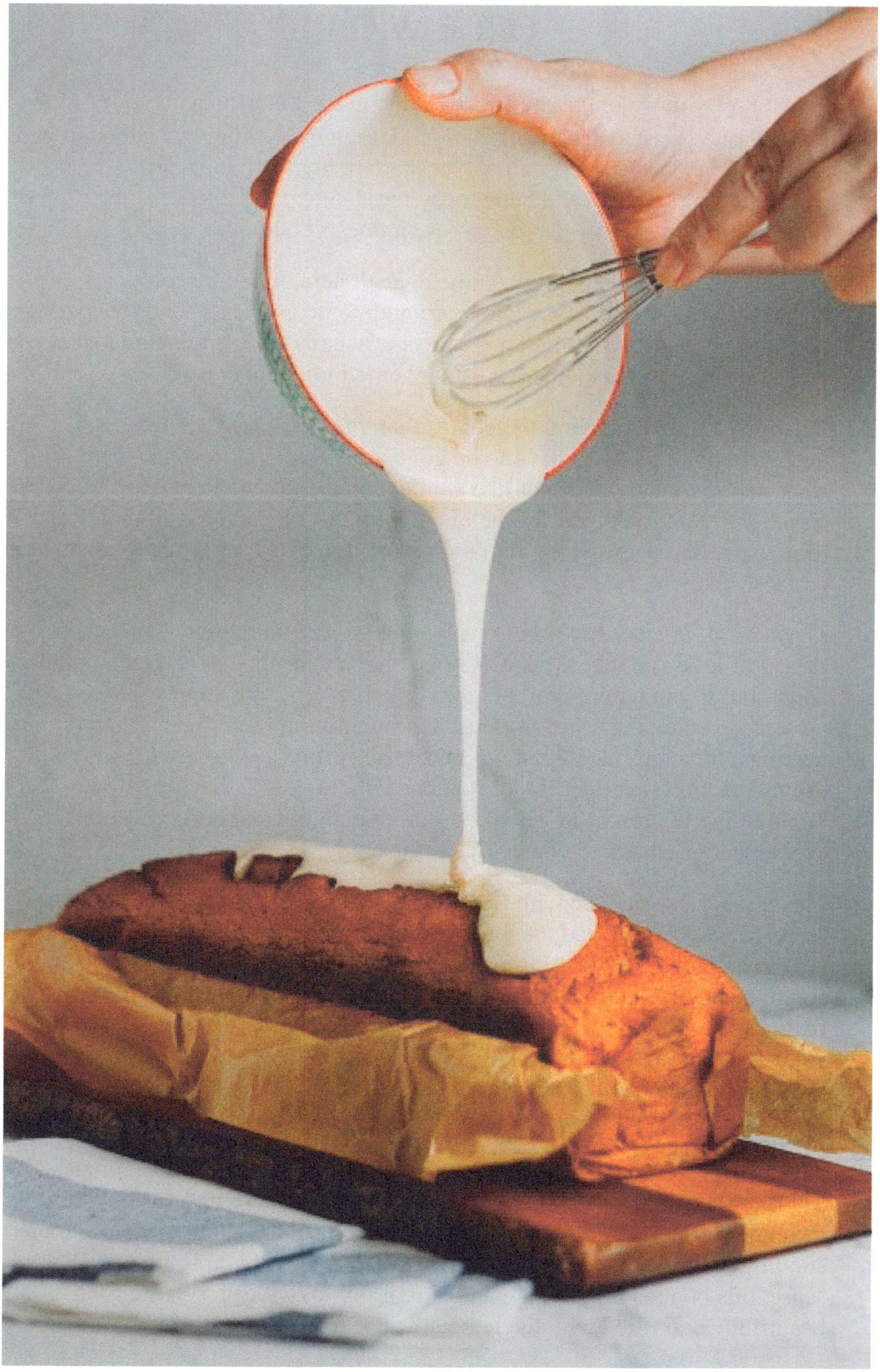

FOREWORD

Right now I'm watching my friend Annie in the kitchen trying to fix a sauce for her roasted asparagus, and it's taking everything I've got to sit here and write this instead of running over there to help her do it. That's how much I love cooking -- and being nosy too, I suppose. I'll rush at the drop of a hat to stick my spoon in a dish where it doesn't belong.

But that's not really the point. Annie doesn't actually enjoy cooking so much. She doesn't think she knows enough to be good at it, and it leaves her defeated. Even at the helm of a recipe, she usually ends up feeling lost. And yet, here she is in the kitchen, creating something delicious.

The thing I'm really trying to get at is that you don't have to love cooking as much as I do. You don't have to be good at it. You don't even have to know what you're doing either, but like Annie, you do have to be willing to give it a shot. Perhaps you'll learn something along the way and have fun doing it (or maybe, like many of my first recipes, it'll just be a giant mess, and that's perfectly okay too!)

The heart of this book is simple; you eat with your eyes first. The visual appeal of food is our first taste. You can have your flavors and technique down, but if you ignore presentation, it feels like an unwrapped birthday present -- something's just missing. For me, nothing feels better than making a delicious meal, plating it beautifully, and seeing my friends so excited about it that they HAVE to take a photo before they take a bite. Taking time to present food makes it more enticing and builds the excitement of what's to come. That's the magic of eye candy!

The garnishes I grew up with aren't going to be the ones you'll find in this book. Maybe you've had them too: wilted kale leaves with an orange slice next to an omelet, a pile of mint and a maraschino cherry on a whipped cream cloud, a wad of parsley on top of a bowl of chowder. I'm not saying these timeless classics taste bad or can't be used -- they do add a dash of color and freshness. But I'm going for something new, a garnish that's exciting and interesting, both visually and to the palate.

I hope that this book will inspire you to explore the endless possibilities and creations that can be made using simple ingredients and easy techniques. My role is not so much to teach you how to use tools or develop advanced techniques, but rather to encourage you to pursue those things in your own cooking journey and give you some inspiration to get you started. In that sense, this book is more of a manifesto of my love for presenting food beautifully and filled with the lessons I've learned along the way.

Whatever the occasion, this book will help you to create a culinary experience to remember. If you feel like my friend in the kitchen struggling with her asparagus, I'm here to teach you what you need to be confident in your skills as a home chef. In the next chapters, you'll learn how to select ingredients for garnishes and about what it takes to craft a perfect dish.

You'll also get a spread of visual inspiration for plating ideas you can do yourself. I'm not a professional, but I have found what's tried and true for me in my cooking and garnishing experience and that is what I'm going to share with you.

With that, you're officially invited to garnish with me! So grab your chef hat, have fun, & make a mess.

You have my permission.

- xx pia

TABLE OF CONTENTS

◊ ◊ ◊

Introduction…10
The Vision…14
Tools…20
How to Prepare…24
Garnishing Dictionary…26
Categories…28
Gathering Ingredients…68
Techniques…72
Pairing Flavors & Textures…79
Plating Your Dish…86
Cultivating an Experience…91
Simple Recipes…94
Conclusion…108
Notes…109
Photographers…111
About…112

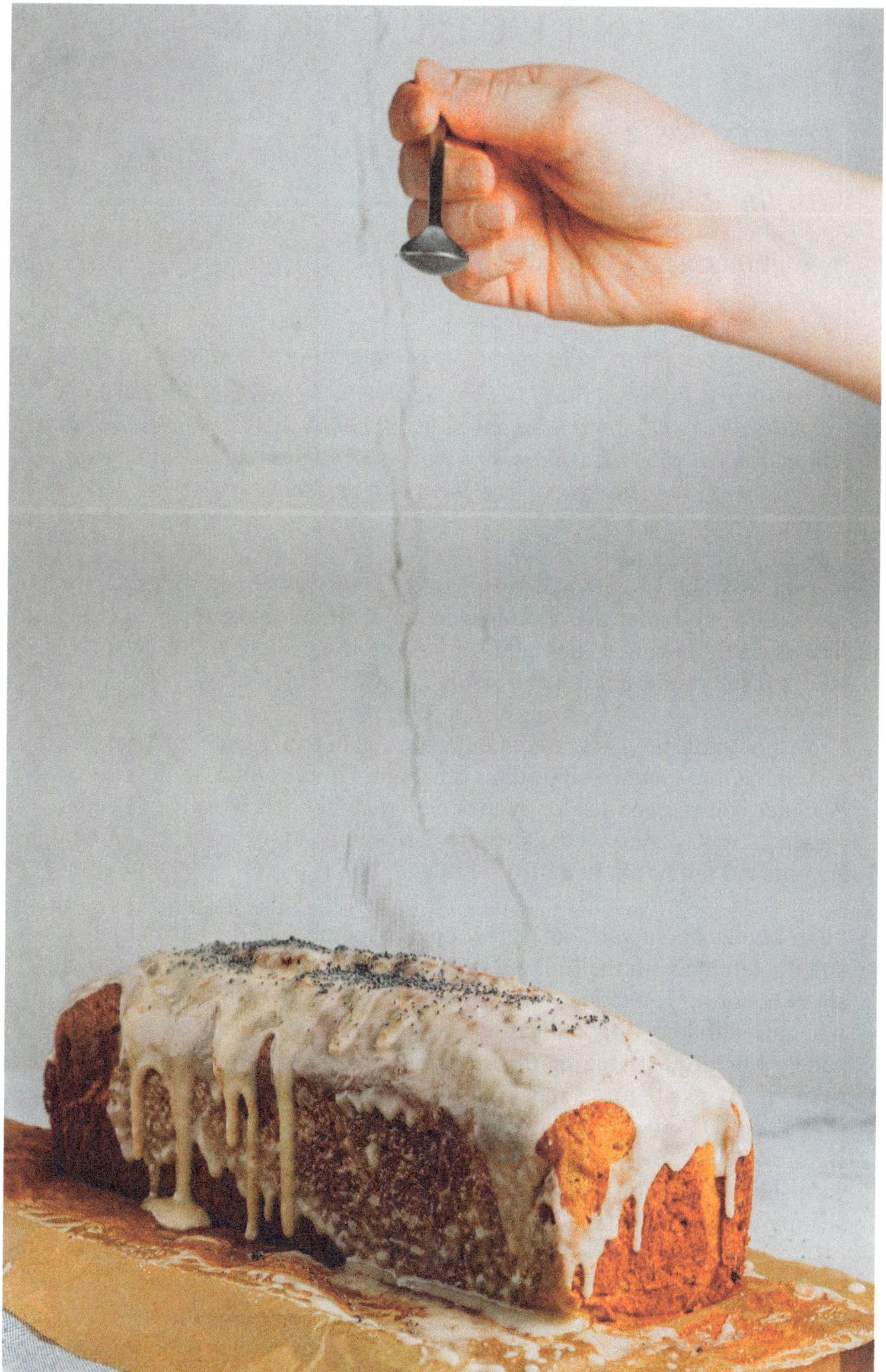

INTRODUCTION

"The first taste is always with the eyes."

- Francesco Leonardi, *Apicius*

Remember what I said about eye candy earlier? Well, there it is, 1st century A.D. baby. Food is sexy. Seriously. It's seductive before it's anything else (well, good food anyways). It captivates the senses, draws you in with scent, visuals, vapors, and flavors. And, just like a dating profile, everybody has their own preferences.

In a sense, when you create a dish, you're really just dressing it up for a hot date with your dinner guest. You spend hours picking the recipe, getting the flavors right, making it look good, adjusting things here and there until you're ready to present the end result.

The art of garnishing is really about creating an experience for your guest, something that touches all of their senses and invites them to the table. Whether you're making sloppy joes or coq au vin, it's worthy of being presented with dignity. That's where garnishing comes in! It's the first thing anyone will notice about a dish.

I don't know about you, but I grew up as a member of the Clean Plate Club, and it's left me with the lifelong belief that there is something important about honoring your food. There are many interpretations of that, but to me, it begins with knowing and valuing where your food comes from (and the people who grew it), taking time to cook something delicious, or as simple as saying thanks before a meal.

Before we start, there are a few basic ground rules you have to know about garnishing. The culinary world takes stuff like this pretty seriously -- as I'm writing this, I just watched a team on a competitive cooking show get kicked off for serving their food with an inedible garnish (in this case, a chunk of coral). Of course, we aren't all under the scrutiny of world-class chefs, but these three basic rules are important for expert and home chefs alike, so make sure to check each box for every garnish you make. So there you go, rule number one:

1. *Never serve an inedible garnish.* Just don't do it, k? Garnishes have to be functional. If they're not consumable, or if they don't serve a practical purpose (shish kebab skewers and toothpick parasols are great for keeping a garnish together), they don't belong on the plate.

2. *Garnishes enhance the star of the dish.* Think of your main ingredient and go from there. The garnish should complement the primary ingredient and play to the overall flavor of the dish. You want to avoid overpowering the flavors you've worked hard to produce in your culinary creation, but you don't want to play it too safe and risk your dish's flavor falling flat. It's all about balance!

3. *Garnishes add complexity & contrast.* It goes without saying; nobody likes a boring, underseasoned dish. To add some complexity and contrast to your dish, you will need some understanding of what flavors and textures work nicely together. A pinch of salt in your caramel or a spicy kick of red pepper flakes on pasta are both easy examples of this.

You want to create as much sensory interest as you can without jeopardizing rules one and two. If you've got an idea for a garnish or how you want to plate your food, try it out, experiment, and find what works for you.

If you're having trouble getting motivated, here are some quick ideas:

- *Invite your friends over to cook and taste-test.*

- *Grab a sketchbook and scribble out some ideas for a dish you want to make.*

- *Watch an episode of a cooking show that makes you want to run to the kitchen.*

- *Buy yourself some pretty plates or plant a potted kitchen herb garden.*

- *Pretend it's your birthday and bake a cake.*

- *Find a piece of artwork you want to recreate with food.*

- ❖ *Choose a recipe with an ingredient you've never had before.*

- ❖ *Plan a party and cook the food for it.*

- ❖ *Have a date night and treat yourself to your favorite food.*

If you're worried about messing up, don't be; every attempt will teach you something new. If you make something you don't think turned out well, learn from it and move on. It's not about being perfect, it's about enjoying your time in the kitchen and bringing your culinary vision into reality.

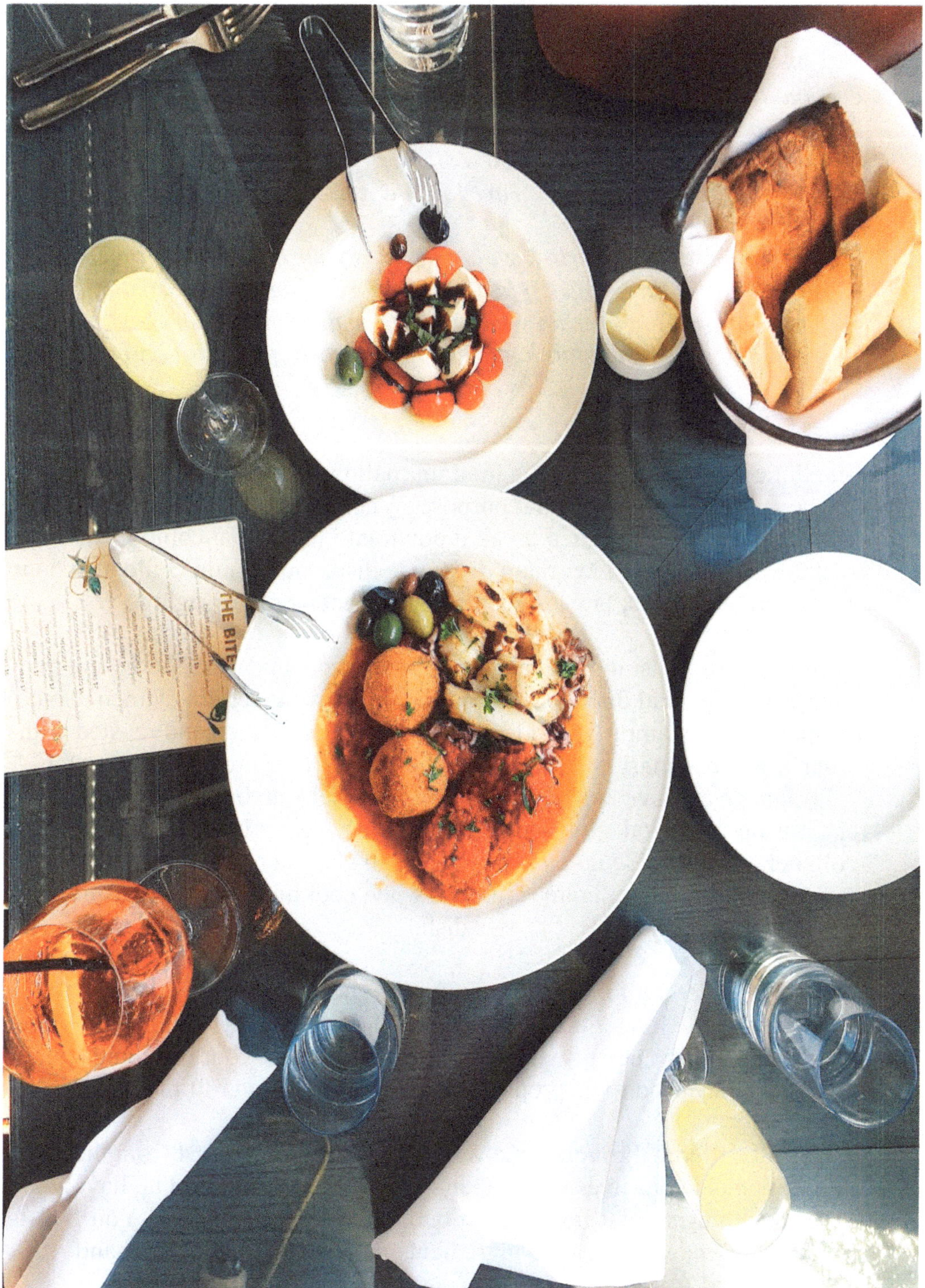

THE VISION

This is the ideation part of garnishing. Before you begin cooking and eventually plating, it's a great idea to think about how you want to present your dish. What do you want it to look like? You could recreate a famous work of art, express a feeling, tell a story, or just plain wing it: the options are infinite.

Think of yourself as an artist, with a plate as your canvas and food as the medium. To take that one step further, be more of a makeup artist of sorts. Your job isn't to cover up your subject (or food in this case) beyond recognition but is instead to honor the uniqueness of the dish and show off its best features.

One thing that has helped me is food journaling. I keep a sketchbook in my kitchen with a pen just for that purpose. When I come up with an idea, I'll sketch the final dish and then break it down into individual components. The breakdown could look like: main dish, side dish, sauce. You could also do it by protein, carbs, fats, or even color -- whatever feels right to you.

From there, I'll list ingredients as well as flavors and qualities I want to bring out in the final dish. I take notes on how I want certain elements to be composed. An example could look like, "Potatoes: halved and roasted with garlic and rosemary, served beside the steak." This process is great for bringing a creative element to cooking and helps to build a thoughtful relationship with food. Not to mention, if you've got a helper in the kitchen, collaborating on these notes beforehand can get you on the same page and give you both something to reference when cooking separate parts of the dish.

The other reason for planning your idea ahead of time is that certain garnishes require longer prep time. For some garnishes, you'll have to have them made in advance of whenever you plan to cook your dish, and some may need to be prepared hours or days ahead of time.

We've all suffered through some wilted greens or burnt toast from the last-minute cooks in our lives (mom that's you), but you may end up having to serve something similar if you don't budget your time properly! You'll also want to know if there are ingredients you need to buy beforehand.

It's easy to overthink garnishing, so try to stay present and just enjoy the moment. Food is beautiful on its own, and if you present it thoughtfully it won't need anything fancy. Garnishing is that delicate final touch which wraps everything together into one cohesive dish.

When I first thought of the title for this book, I didn't know what "visual guide" meant. All I knew was that I was tired of reading walls of text to figure out something a picture could tell me. Humans are sensory creatures, after all. We all have fond memories of garnishes, whether it's picking herbs from your mother's garden, tying a knot in a maraschino cherry stem with your tongue, icing cookies in preparation for Santa Claus, or rushing to add all the birthday candles before the guests arrive. It shapes cultures, traditions, holidays, families, relationships, you name it. That's why I think garnishing is so important-- if you eat with your eyes first, that's half the experience.

Cabernet Sauvignon
Chianti
Rhône to Pauillac w/ Cabernet
Arugula salad
w/ shallot & red wine vinaigrette
glazed pears w/ Honey
roasted chicken w/ rosemary
Chianti wine sauce
puréed
butternut squash (or acorn)
Chianti Sauce
Sage rosemary & bay
Chianti classico
olive oil
Garlic
broth

CASE STUDY

Here is a snapshot of the kind of sketches I create in my kitchen before I make a dish. This was my take on a fall dinner: roasted chicken with herbs, puréed butternut squash, grilled pears with a honey glaze, and a side salad with arugula, roasted squash seeds, pomegranate seeds, tossed with a simple shallot vinaigrette, and a drizzle of chianti wine sauce. I used a large round white plate and arranged the foods in a spiral shape with the chicken and pear as the focal points. The functional garnishes of this dish are the squash seeds, pomegranate seeds, and the drizzle of chianti wine sauce. The squash purée adds a contrasting texture alongside the chicken, pear, and the salad. All of the flavors are using produce that is in season, so I know that I'll have the freshest ingredients with the best taste.

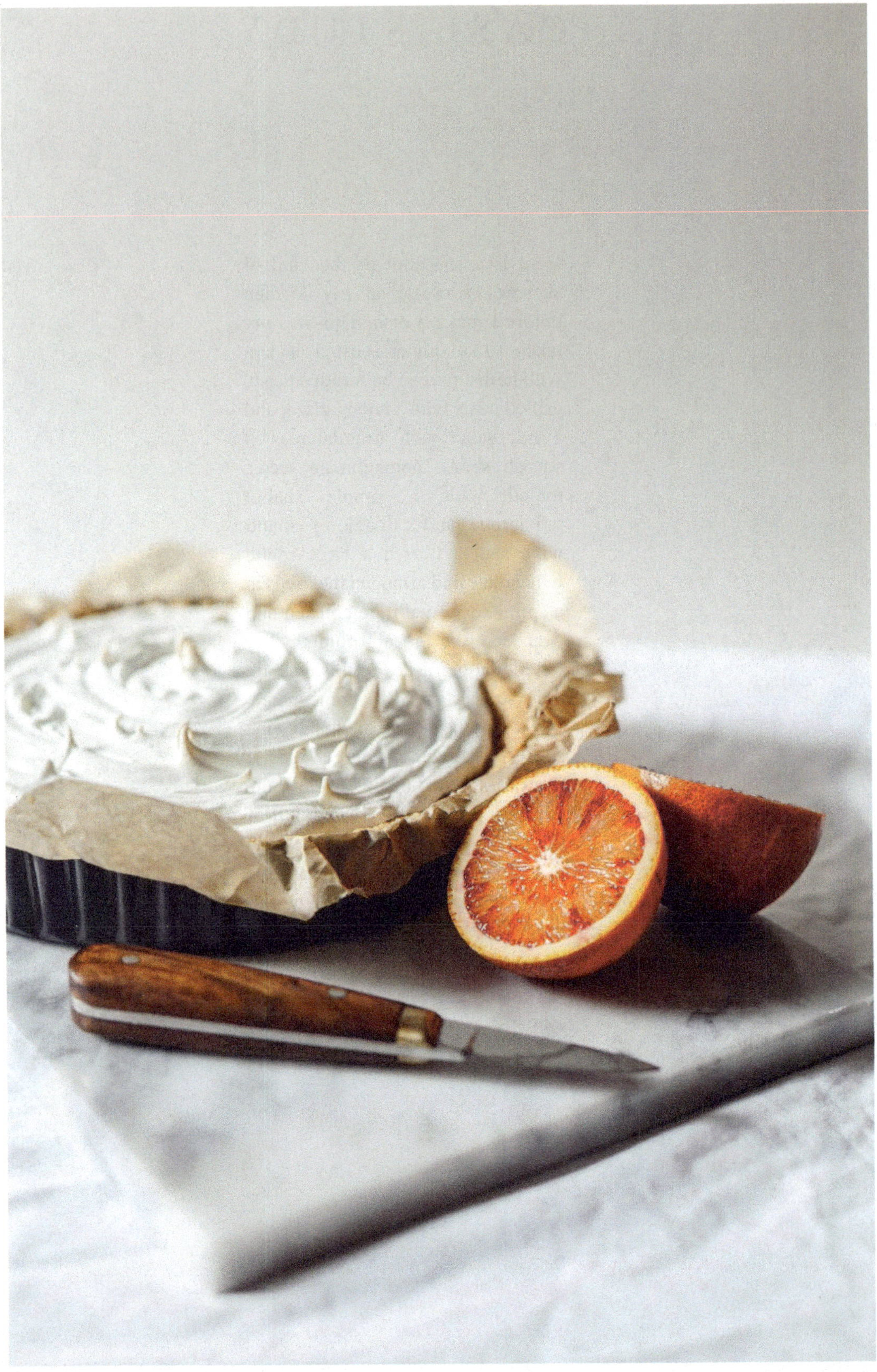

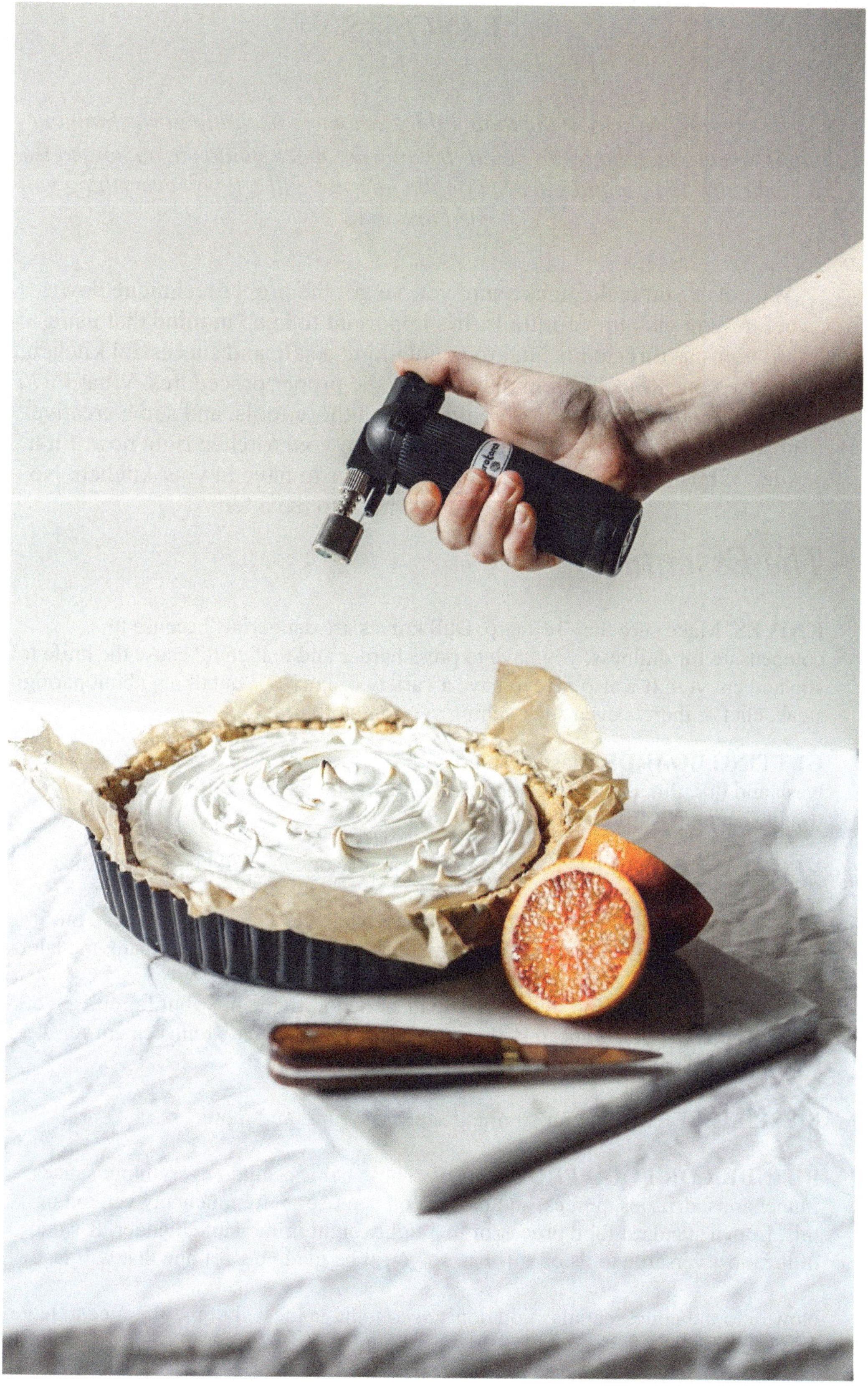

TOOLS

This section will cover the tools I think are most useful in garnishing but won't discuss techniques in detail. If you want more guidance on how to use a particular tool, a quick search on the internet will tell you everything you need to know.

Whatever you make, make sure you've got the proper technique down before you pick up your tools. It's important to keep in mind that using these items as directed is vital to maintaining a safe and successful kitchen, so please consult instruction manuals for the proper procedures. What I *will* be teaching you is what you could do with those tools, and some creative substitutions for tools you might not have in your kitchen right now. First order of business; here are the tools you have to have in your kitchen. No buts about it, you just have to have 'em.

The Essentials

KNIVES Make sure they're sharp. Dull knives are dangerous because to compensate for dullness, you have to press harder and that could cause the knife to slip and cut you. It's also nice to have a variety of knives. I'm talking about paring, steak, chef's; there's even such a thing as a tomato knife!

CUTTING BOARDS Plastic can go in the dishwasher, wood you'll have to hand wash and dry. Put a slightly damp towel underneath the board if you're having trouble keeping it from sliding around.

VEGETABLE PEELER Choose a good quality one. You'll be glad you did.

ZESTER In a pinch you could finely mince whatever you wanted to zest, but if you're planning on doing this often, please just buy a zester. You'll thank me later.

MELON BALLER You might not use this one too frequently, but I promise you that the one time you *do* need it, there really isn't an adequate replacement for it with stuff you can find lying around the house.

MESH SIEVE Needed for straining sauces, syrups, and more.

BLENDER OR FOOD PROCESSOR These babies can do everything: sauces, immersions, drizzles, purées, and more. You can use pretty much any version of this, from a standard food processor to a lightweight immersible blender. It's one of the most versatile tools on this list, so you'll be glad you got one that will last.

Now onto the nonessentials. You don't *need* to have these, but they're nice to have in the kitchen.

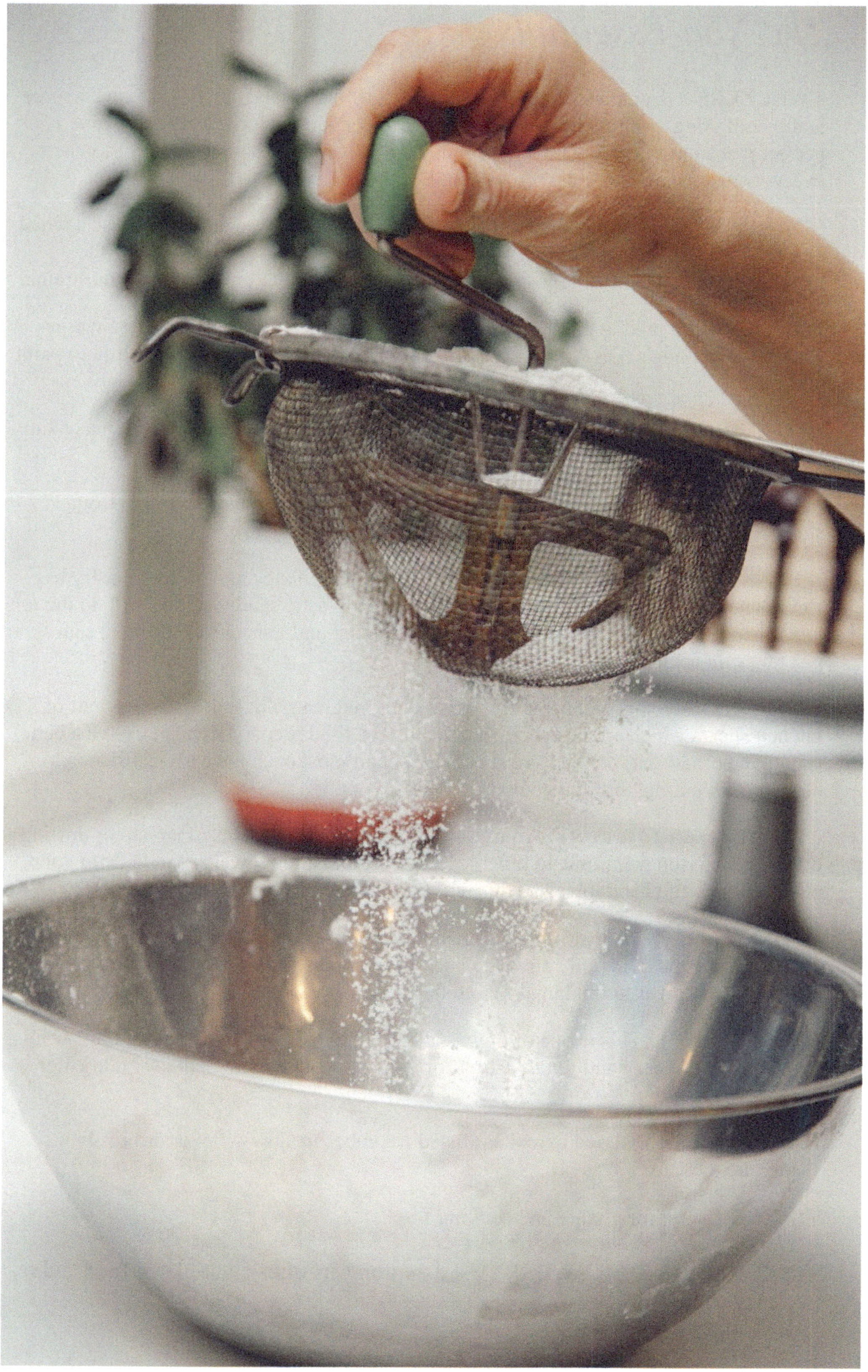

The Non-Essentials

TWEEZERS Okay, these ones are really just for fun. But seriously you can do some really cool things with them. There's nothing like a good pair of tweezers to give you perfect precision for your garnished creations! Also doesn't having a pair of kitchen tweezers just make you feel... professional?

SIFTER If a recipe calls for sifted flour and you don't have one, you can use a whisk or a big fork to fluff up the flour. For creating a 'dusting' effect, you can put the dusting material into an empty spice jar with a perforated lid or use a mesh tea strainer.

BRUSH We're talking pastry brush here. You can use it for things like egg washes on pastries or soaking cakes with syrups, the options are limitless and it's just fun to paint your food.

PAINT BRUSH A fantastic tool to use for detailing food and desserts but make sure they're food-safe.

METAL STRAW Great for serving with drinks and even to use as fruit cut-out stencils.

A PLASTIC BAG/PASTRY BAG If you want to be fancy and go for a pastry bag, I'm not stopping you. But if you aren't that type, a plastic sandwich bag will do the job just fine. It's a great thing to have for piping frosting and ganache or dips and sauces. It just takes things up a notch.

SCISSORS Scissors are so multipurpose, they're great. You can also get a pair of kitchen shears which are designed specifically for food preparation. They have a better grip than normal scissors, they're super sharp, and most even have a specific notch designed for cutting through poultry joints.

CLOTH TOWEL A towel is so useful for cleaning up the sides of a plate or dusting off the countertop from time to time. Keep your garnishing towel separate from your plain old dish and hand towels -- this will keep it clean and make it last.

WHISK There are many different kinds, but you can stick with whatever one you can get your hands on. Did you know you can buy miniature whisks too? They're so fun and especially great for making vinaigrettes or sauces.

BLOW TORCH This is one of those cool kitchen gadgets that everybody just wants to have. They're easy and fun to use, surprisingly cheap, and immediately add color and flavor to food.

ICE CUBE TRAY Used to make infused ice cubes to slowly flavor drinks. Fun shapes are a bonus!

TONGS Useful for plating and cooking food.

TOOTHPICKS & SKEWERS Used to prop garnishes on drinks or food and to make kebab-style dishes.

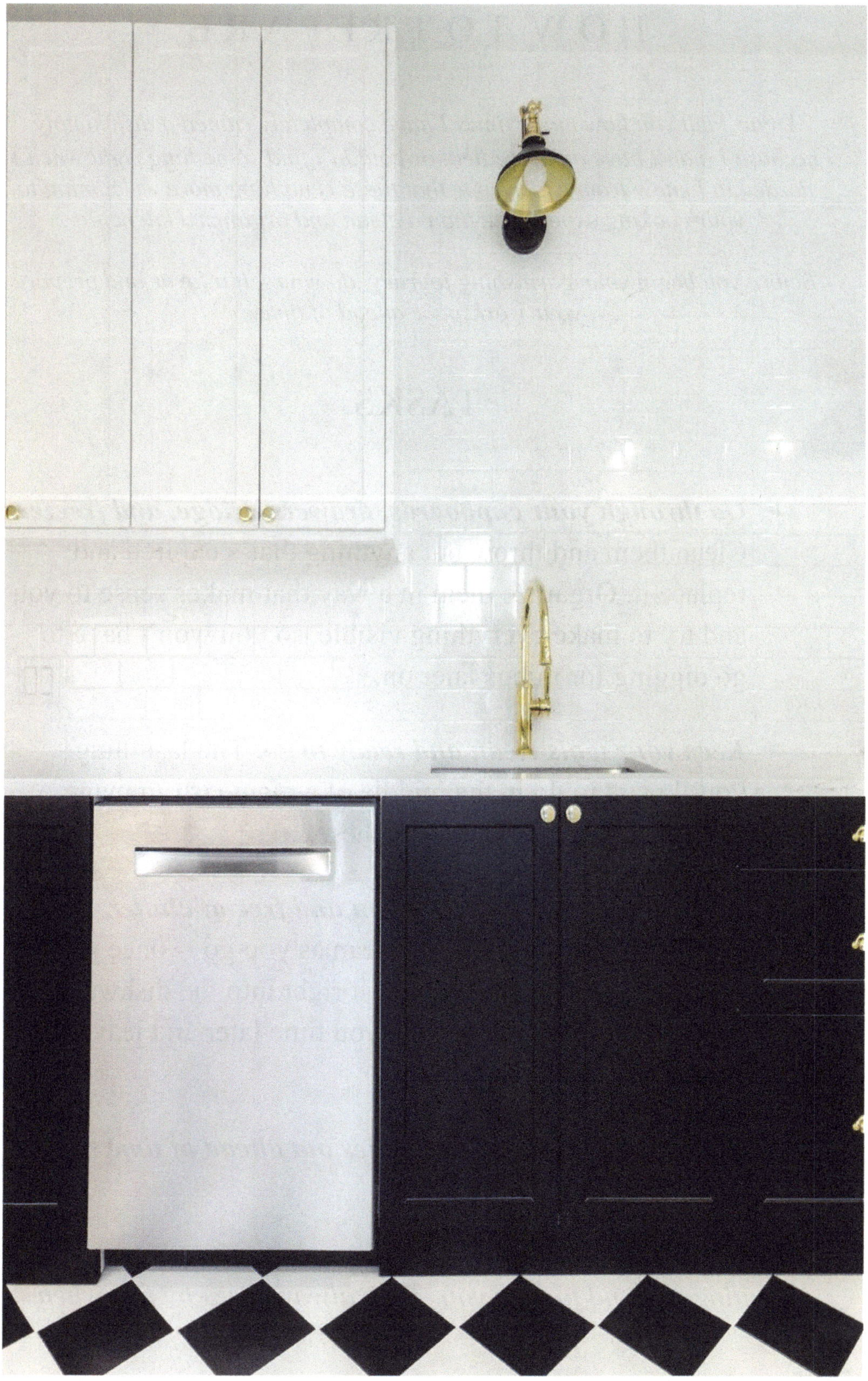

HOW TO PREPARE

I can't tell you how many times I have completely ruined a dish simply because I didn't have an ingredient or couldn't find something right when I needed it. I know from experience that there is nothing more welcoming to your cooking experience than a clean and organized kitchen!

Before you begin your garnishing journey, do yourself a favor and prepare your workspace ahead of time.

TASKS

- ***Go through your cupboards, drawers, fridge, and freezer.*** Clean them and throw out anything that's expired and replace it. Organize them in a way that makes sense to you and try to make everything visible, so you won't have to go digging for things later on.

- ***Keep your tools clean and ready to go.*** The last thing you'll want to do in the middle of a recipe is rummage through a sink full of dirty dishes.

- ***Keep your work surfaces clean and free of clutter.*** It'll help you out later on if you clean as you go -- once you're done using a tool or dish, pop it right into the dishwasher or clean it in the sink to save you time later and leave your workspace clear.

- ***Plan your dishes and garnishes out ahead of time*** so you don't have to rush.

TIP: *If you need help focusing, try putting on some music or inviting a friend to help you. Time always goes by fast when you're having fun!*

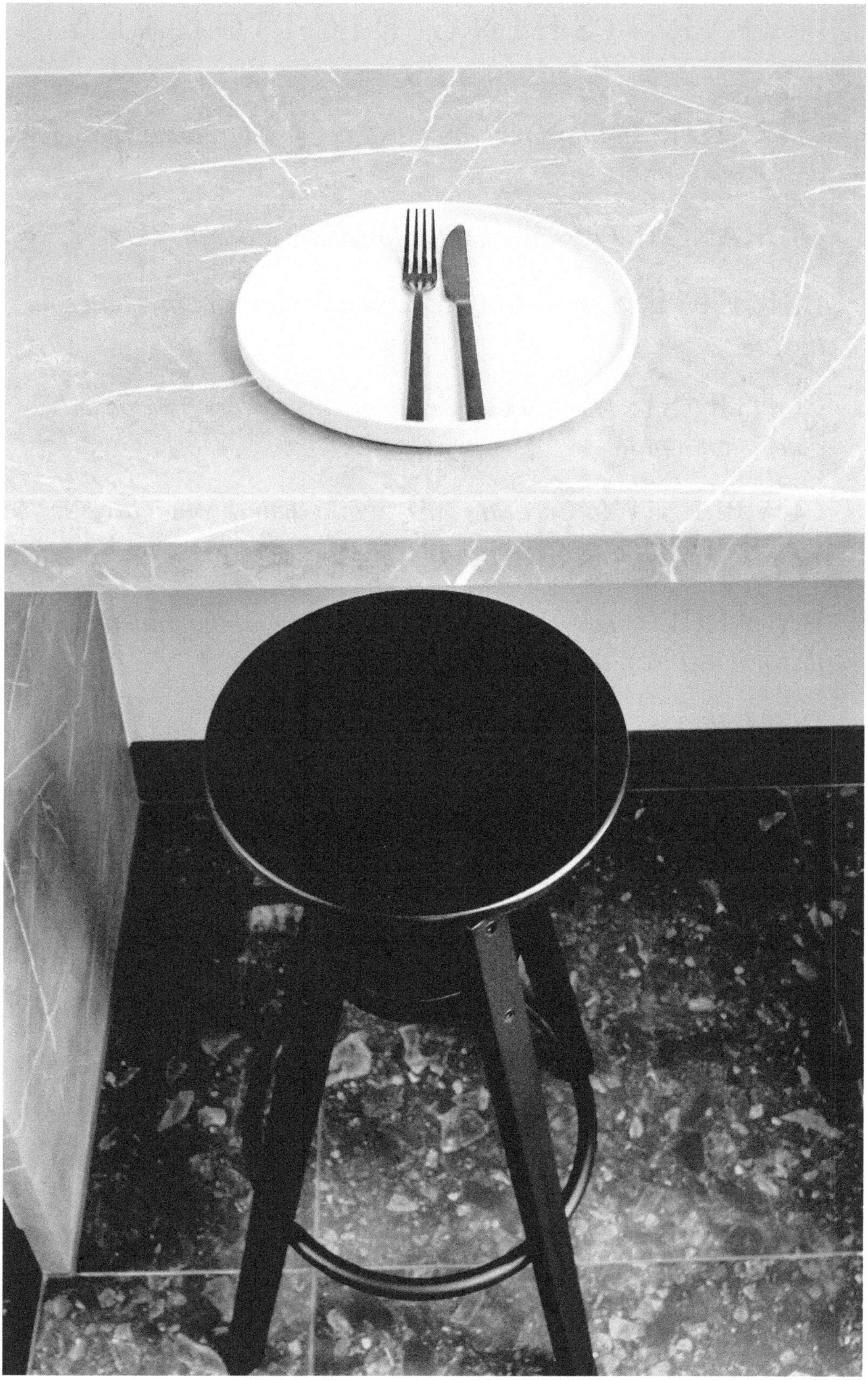

GARNISHING DICTIONARY

GARNISH: *An ingredient or substance used as decoration for a dish or drink*

VIBRANCY: *Freshness and color of the food, the 'life'*

BRIGHTNESS: *In reference to visual color, acidity, and sour flavors.*

CONTRAST: *The stark difference between two juxtaposed objects on a plate*

COMPLEXITY: *Creating variety in a dish through diverse flavors and textures*

BALANCE: *The symmetry and asymmetry of the plated dish, flavors, textures, or subsequent qualities of food*

COLOR: *The brain associates different colors with different types of food, flavors, and smells*

FLAVOR: *How the brain interprets food based on aromas, taste, and mouthfeel*

TASTE: *The interpretation of food from the tongue to the brain*

MOUTHFEEL: *The physical sensations in the mouth created by a food*

TEXTURE: *Properties of food sensed by physical touch or felt by the hands or mouth*

ELEMENTS: *The components of a dish consisting of the main dish, complementary elements or sides, sauces, and garnishes*

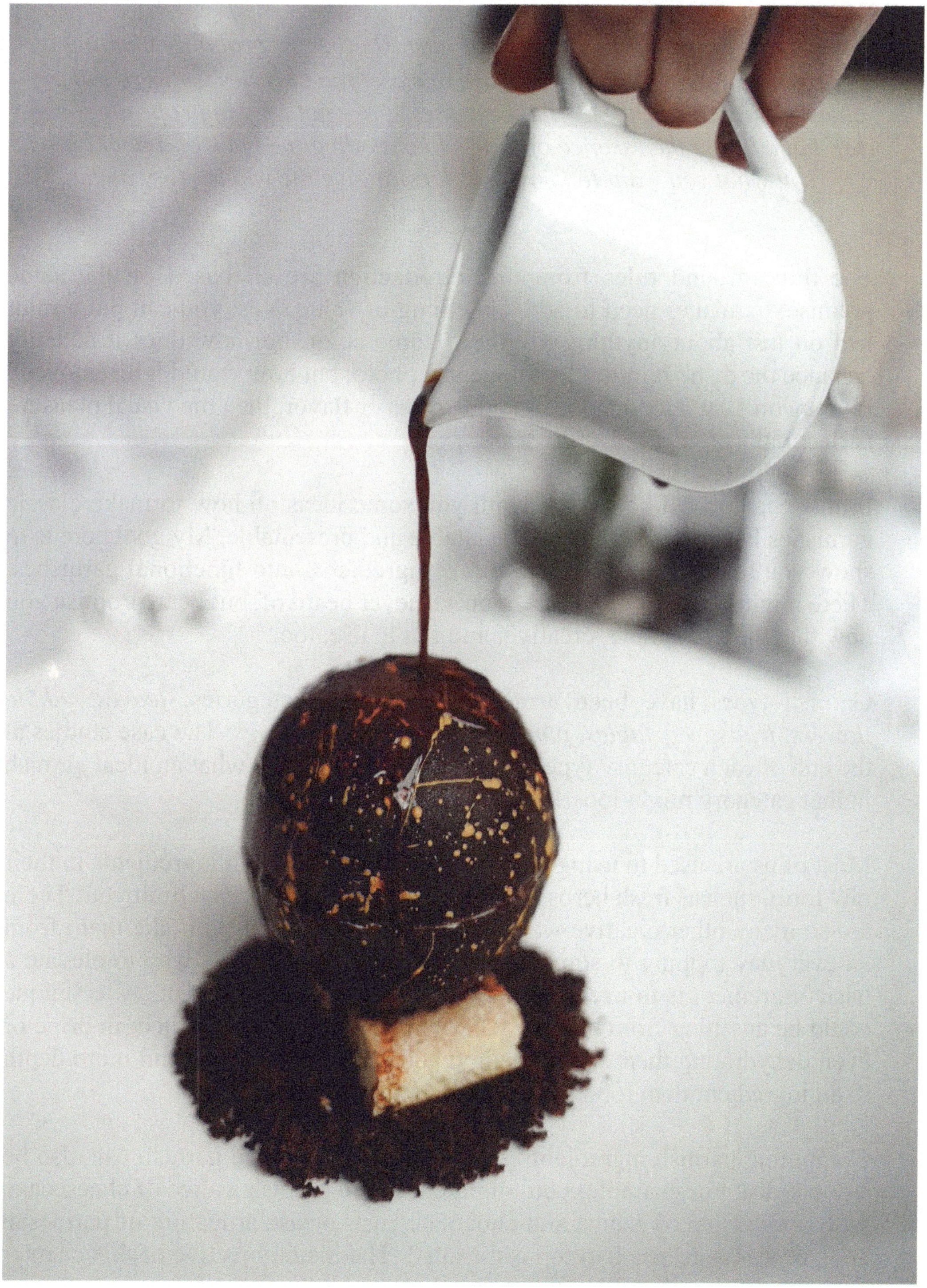

CATEGORIES

When most people hear the word garnish, they're probably thinking of sprigs of mint and parsley or those maraschino cherries we were talking about earlier. Garnishes -- the best ones -- are not only appropriate for the dish but capture the essence of it. It's like reading the back of a book; it tells you what you want to know but doesn't give the whole story away.

The three ground rules from the introduction are all based on the same premise: garnishes need to add something of value. Yes, you can put a mint leaf on just about anything to give it some color, but how does it actually enhance the dish? It might look nice in a photo, but how would it be enjoyed? If you won't eat it, and it doesn't add aroma or flavor, then the visual pleasure is fleeting.

In this chapter, I'll be sharing with you some ideas on how to make classic garnishes like mint leaves more palatable and presentable. My goal here is to show you how to transform these raw ingredients into functional garnishes. There might be some techniques you've never heard of, but I can promise you now that they're simple, creative, and fun to use, too.

Garnish types have been arranged into seven categories: *leaves, edible flowers, fruits, vegetables, purées, drizzles,* and *toppings.* The case studies at the end of each category type will give you insight into what an ideal garnish in that category might look like.

Most of us are used to using garnishes that are made with ingredients in their raw form, such as fresh herbs or sliced fruit, but don't let that limit you! There are so many other creative ways to use ingredients that will take them from an everyday topping to something showstopping. The best way to elevate a basic ingredient is to use a technique that transforms its flavor. A technique could be anything from heating your ingredients to pickling them in brine or even dehydrating them. Each method adds a different flavor and more depth to an ingredient than it possesses in its raw form.

Combining garnish ingredient types to make a complete garnish can also be a good idea. For example, you might choose to garnish a slice of cheesecake with both raspberry sauce and chocolate curls or use a dusting of parmesan and pomegranate seeds to top off a salad. The main objective of this chapter is to get you comfortable with using each type of ingredient so that you can come up with creative ways to use them.

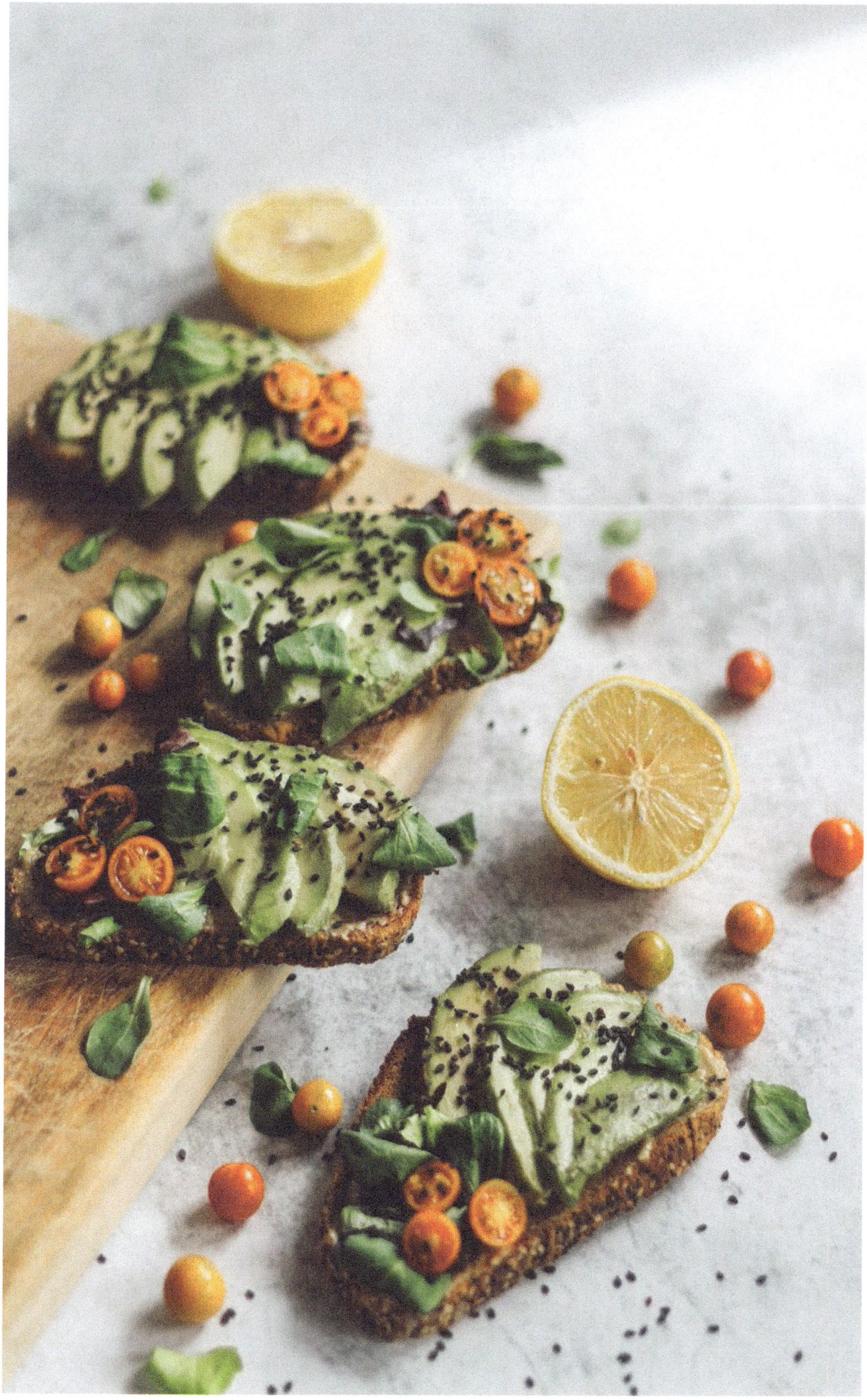

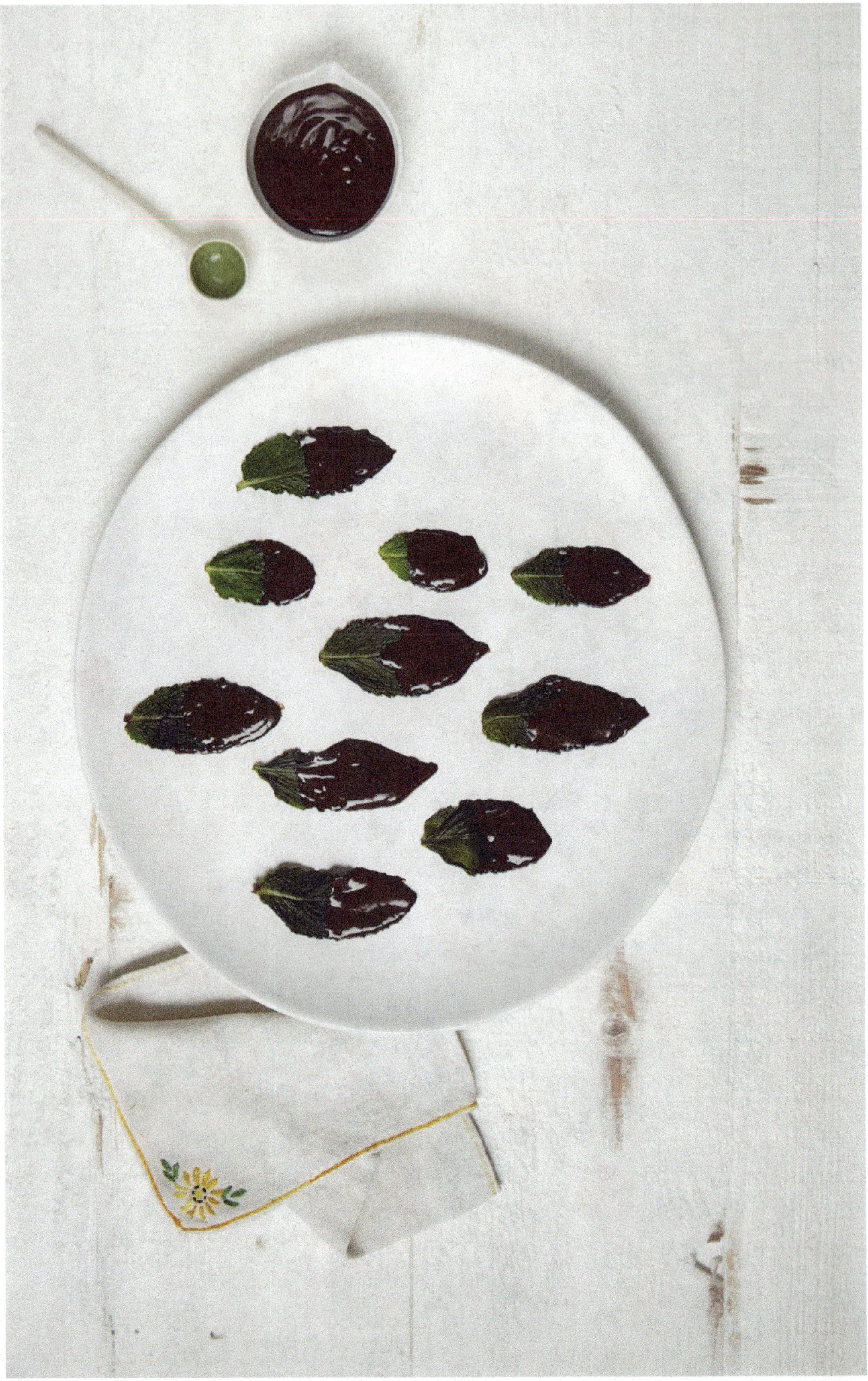

Leaves

(Pictured: chocolate-coated mint leaves)

Leaves are an incredible way to add color and texture if they're presented right. What you don't want to do is leave them as an inedible garnish. Certain leaves can be served in their natural forms, such as microgreens or delicate leafy greens like arugula and basil.

Rougher leaves aren't enjoyable to eat and shouldn't be used to garnish. For example, a kale leaf would not be a palatable garnish in its raw form: it's tough, relatively flavorless, and doesn't add value to the dish like a leaf of spicy arugula or basil would. Making leaves more interesting can be as simple as freezing them into ice cubes with fruits or juice, or even coating them in chocolate.

When you are working with leaves as garnishes, be as gentle as you can to prevent bruising and misshaping the leaves. Storing leaves properly, like all other garnish ingredients, is paramount to making something both beautiful and flavorful.

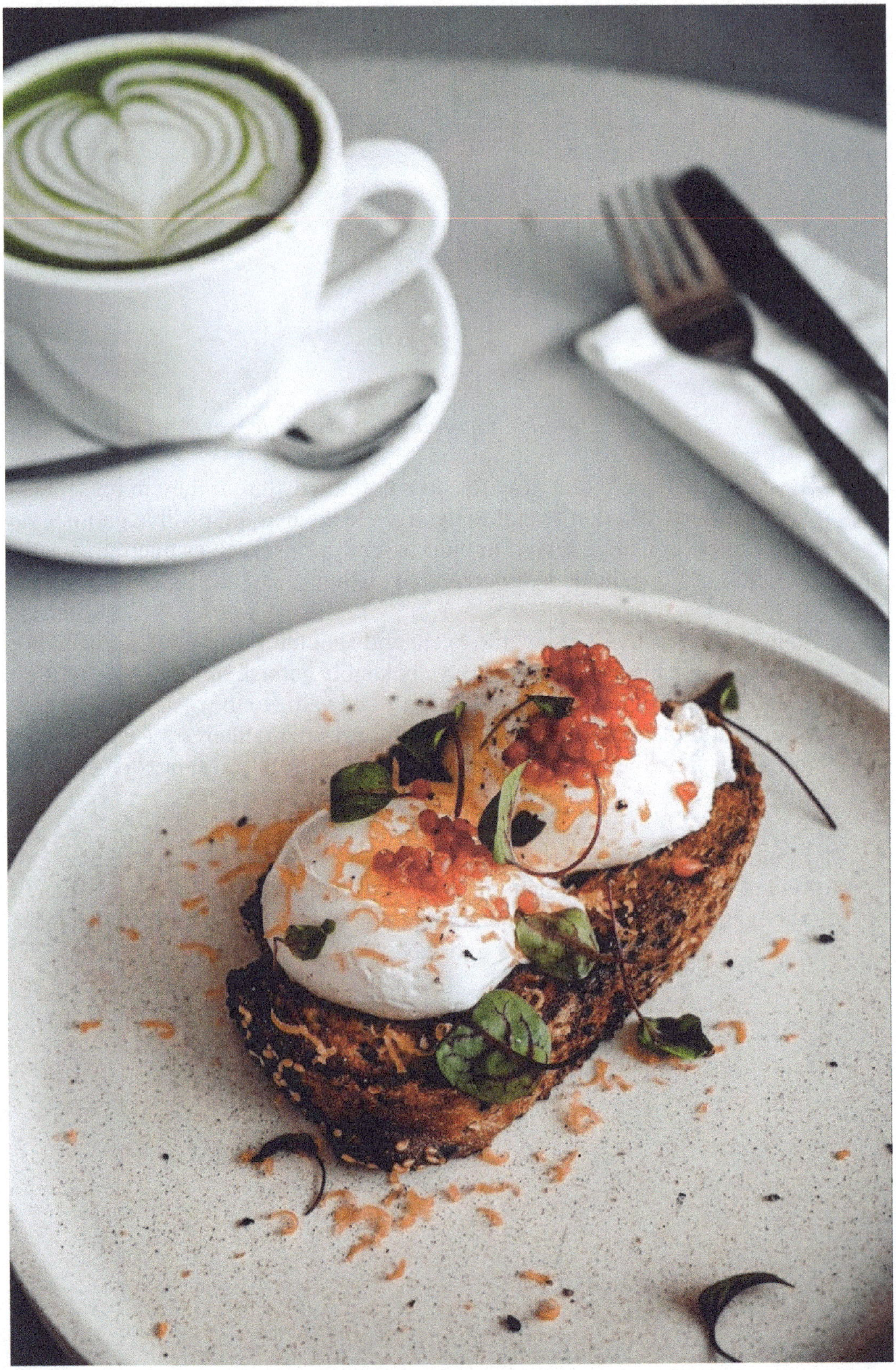

CASE STUDY

(Pictured: roe on poached egg toast with microgreens) Microgreens are the shoots of your garden variety salad vegetables. These little greens pack a lot of flavor in just a pinch of their tiny leaves. They can be very expensive at the store, and they need to be used quickly once they're purchased. My advice is to grow your own; they only take a few days to sprout and within a week or two you'll have beautiful microgreens to use as garnishes. Arugula, radish, beets, pea shoots, and mustards are great microgreens to start if you're looking to grow your own. They're beautiful and add a crispy texture to whatever you put them on. Each microgreen has a different flavor, so be sure to do your research before you dive in headfirst. The best thing to do is to try all of the microgreens you can so you'll have a better idea of what you want to grow. One of the best places to do this is a farmer's market, since there is almost always a vendor selling microgreens and they'll be more than happy to give you free samples before you make a purchase.

Edible Flowers

(Pictured: a hand holding a lavender bundle)

The urge to put flowers on anything from a smoothie bowl to a cake can be hard to resist; my advice would be to not resist it at all! The key with flowers is to know your varieties and what they work best with.

Do put flowers on things if it makes sense for your dish. Flowers can have unique flavors and colors that marry beautifully with many recipes. There are plenty of amazing things you can make with flowers, and a plethora of edible varieties to choose from.

I'm a fan of stuffed squash flowers and candied flowers, but I also enjoy making syrups or infusions with them, especially lilac flowers. Their fragrance and color are delicate and sophisticated, and if you've got any in your yard be sure to make use of them! Jasmine flowers, rose, hibiscus, tulip, pansy, nasturtium, orange blossom, lavender, and chamomile are also great options. If you really want to capture the flavor or essence of something, syruping is a great technique. It works well with herbs like rosemary too!

Infused syrups can be used for anything from fancy drinks to drizzles on desserts. One of my favorite combinations is orange blossom infused syrup with lemon poppyseed pancakes (refer to page 102 for a simple syrup infusion recipe).

Tip: Try storing your syrups in pretty décor jars. You can buy them online or at craft stores. I also love repurposing dropper-style bottles for this. They make great gifts too!

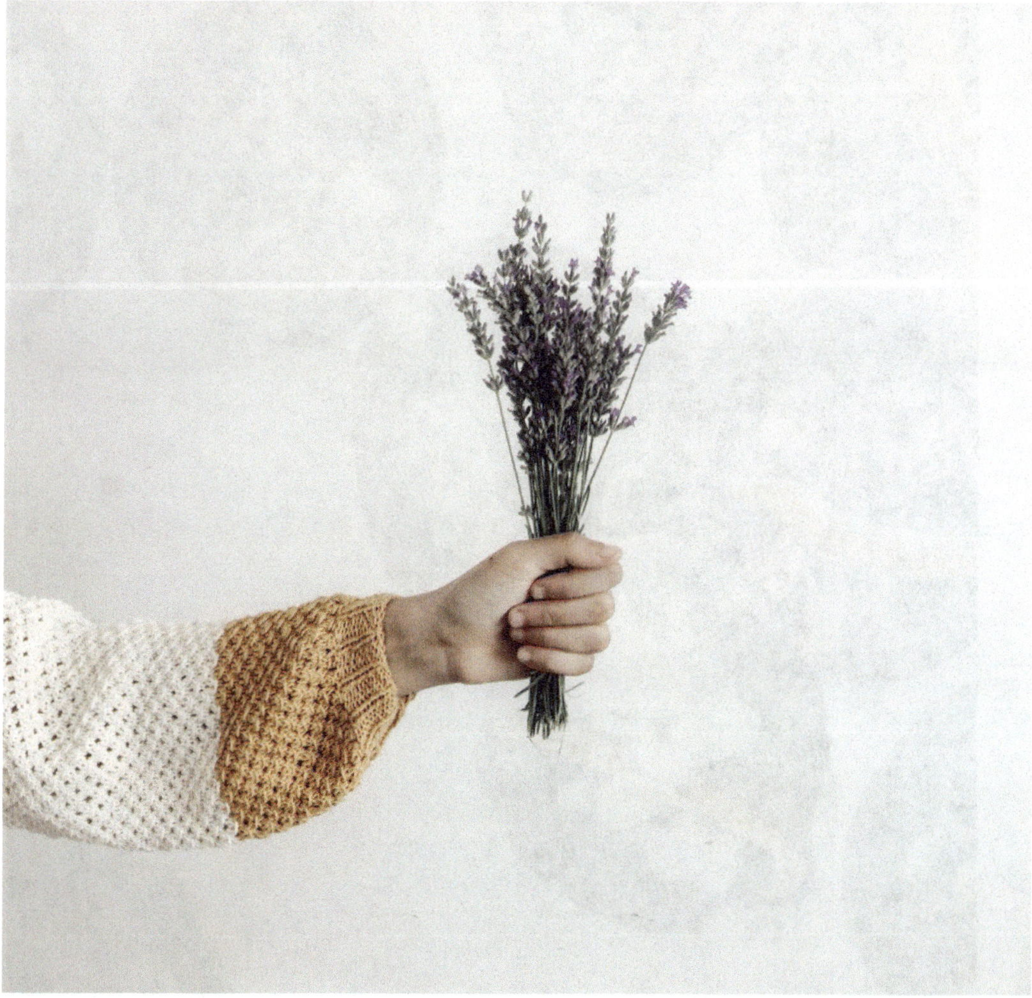

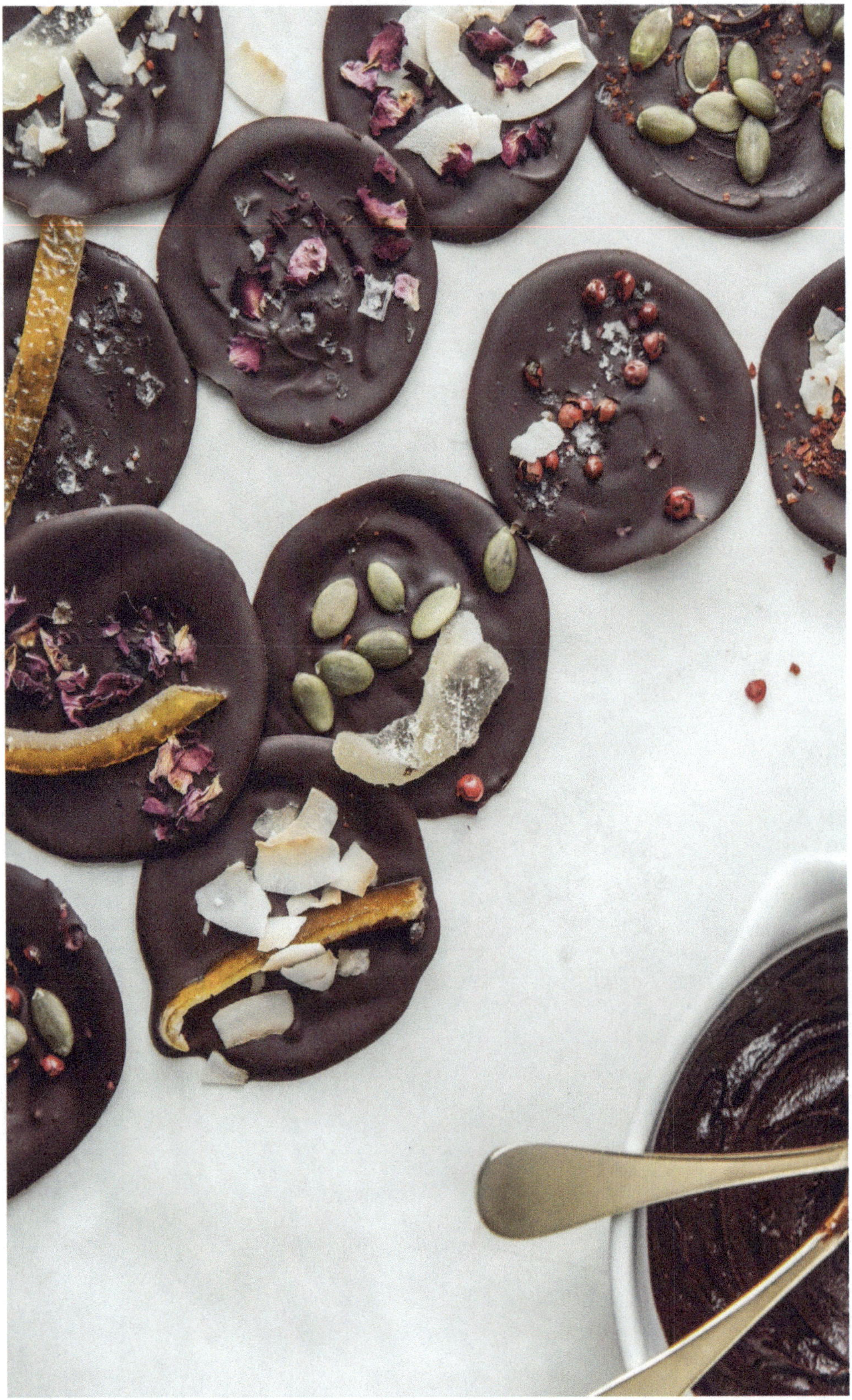

CASE STUDY

Rose petals add mild fragrance, a light flaky texture, and make a great garnish for anything rose-flavored. On my visit to Santa Fe, I tried a whole rainbow of chocolate flavors from chili to coffee and prickly pear, but my favorite was a rose-infused chocolate medallion. The flower petals used in this case were entirely edible and served a purpose more than visual since they indicated the rose-flavored chocolate. What I find a lot of people doing is simply tossing edible flowers on top of just about anything to make it look pretty, which doesn't mean much after you've taken a picture of it. Even if they're edible, most people wouldn't be inclined to eat them unless they're incorporated into the dish in a meaningful way -- and of course only if they taste good. I'm all for flowers if they add something with purpose to the plate, but don't just throw them on there to add color. Do the flowers justice and make them belong there.

CRYSTALLIZED ROSE PETALS

SERVES: 12 | PREP TIME: 3 HOURS

INGREDIENTS

1 oz rose petals
1 egg white
1 cup caster sugar (or fine ground cane sugar)
Parchment paper

DIRECTIONS

Separate your egg and use a fork or whisk to froth the egg white. Use a pair of tweezers to hold a petal while dabbing a light layer of egg white onto it using a paintbrush.

Dust with sugar evenly using a sieve or spoon and rest onto a sheet of parchment paper. Repeat for remaining petals.

Leave flat to dry for at least 2 hours, preferably 8 hours or overnight. Store in an airtight tin between sheets of parchment paper for up to a year.

NOTE: It is important to use caster sugar or a lighter, refined sugar because a traditional granulated will be too heavy for the petals and won't preserve their color or shape as well as superfine will.

Fruits

(Pictured: sliced plums)

They're magical, aren't they? They make just about everything better. You could make jams and jellies, purées, cover them in chocolate, dry them, freeze them, bake them, poach them, preserve them. All of these will make delicious and unique garnishes.

If you're looking to shake things up a bit, try using fruit in a different way. It doesn't have to be anything complicated; simply slicing fruits at a different angle to use as garnishes can add interesting shapes to your plate design.

Tip: Try preserving your fruits in olive oil or quick-pickling them. Lemons in spiced olive oil are a favorite for me, and quick-pickled cherries or grapes are perfect garnishes for tuna salad.

Extra Tip: Have you ever tried shaving apples or pears? They're perfect in salads especially and add an interesting texture and look. To do it, wash your fruits, remove the skins, and use a vegetable peeler to pull gently across to create thin shavings.

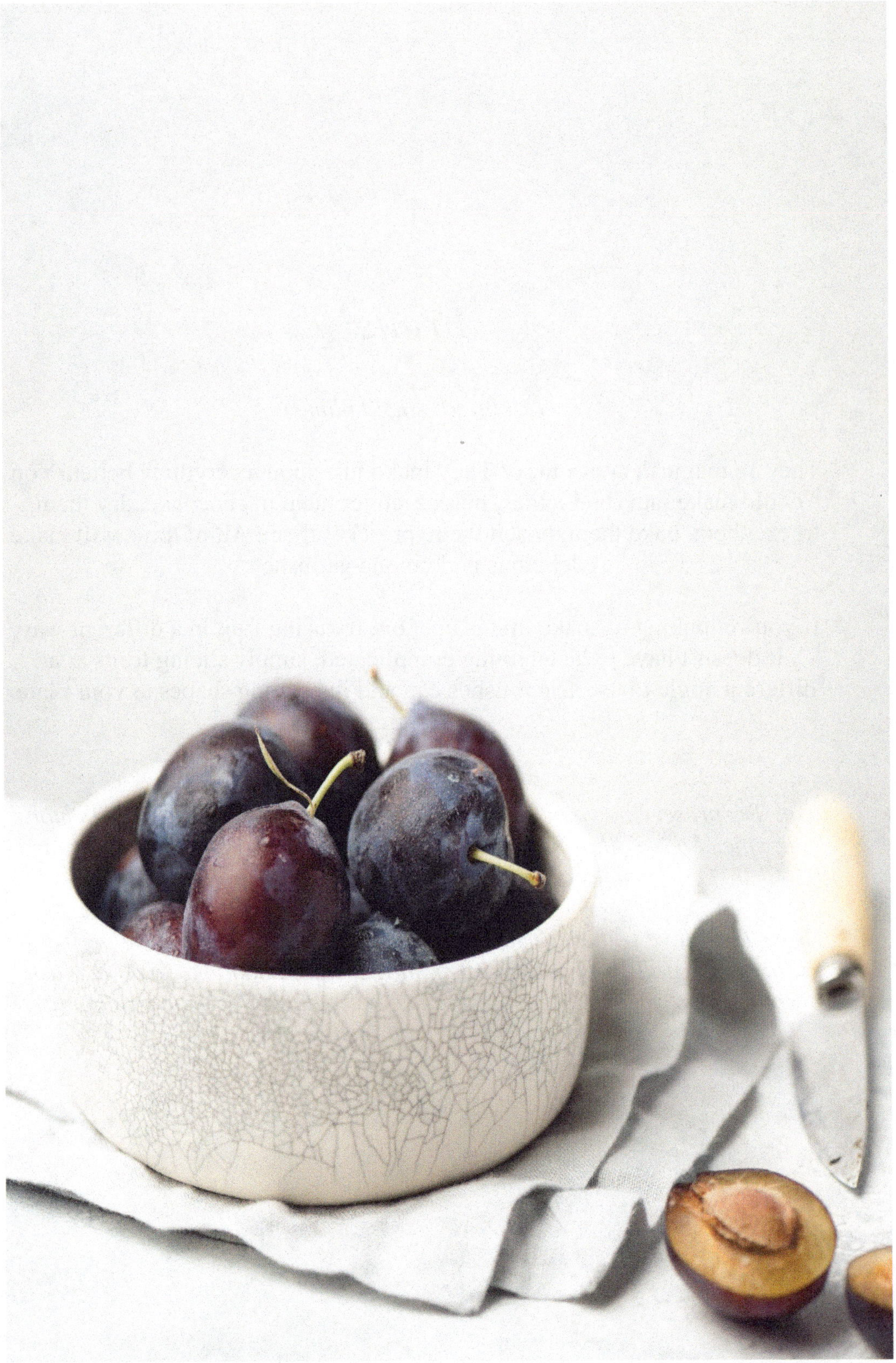

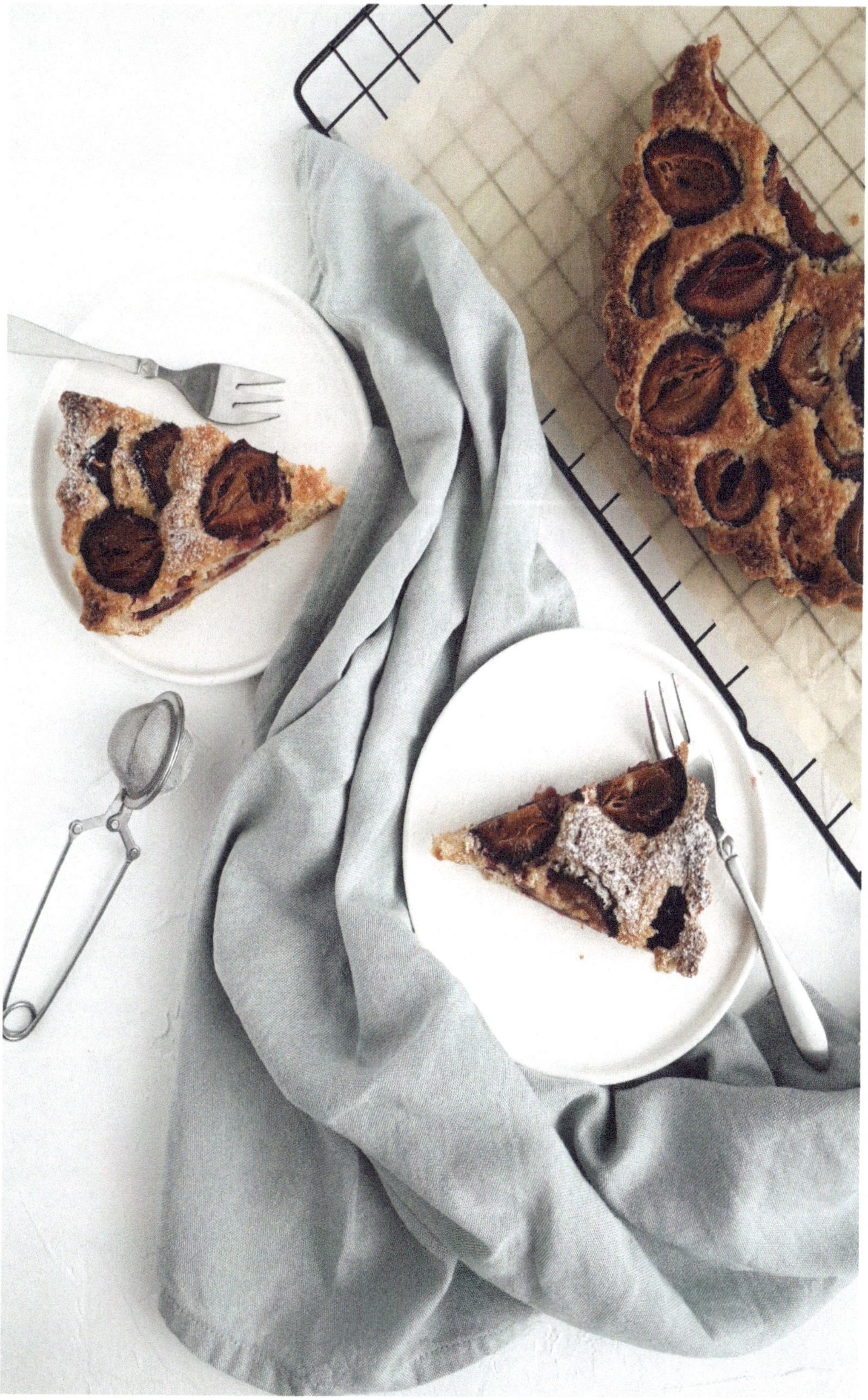

CASE STUDY

(Pictured: sliced plum pie with confectioners sugar) Garnishes don't have to be made from ingredients in their raw forms. In fact, baking your garnishes right into your food or cooking your food in a way that looks more artistic and appealing can create beautiful dishes. Take this plum pie for example; the plums are halved neatly and laid face up to give it an interesting pattern and texture. Once it has been sliced, a simple dusting of confectioners sugar is the perfect thing to polish it into a finished plate. Food really is beautiful all on its own; garnishes are here to take it to the next level but never to outshine the incredible dish you've worked hard to create. Getting good at doing more with less is the ultimate secret to making and garnishing amazing food.

Garnishing Drinks Versus Garnishing Foods

The key difference between garnishing food and garnishing drinks is that there are things you can use to garnish drinks that you can't with food. Take an orange peel for example; it's exactly what a classic old-fashioned needs, but if you try to serve that on a plate of food? Good luck! It won't fly.

Garnishes for food have to be edible -- they shouldn't be something you have to toss to the side while you're eating. Drinks on the other hand can have garnishes that aren't entirely edible. Drinks are meant to be sipped slowly over time, so it's okay to have a garnish like a stem of rosemary that sits in a glass for 15 or 20 minutes and slowly diffuses its flavor, but in the end isn't something that will be eaten directly.

My rule for food garnishes is that if you wouldn't want to pluck it right off the plate and eat it, don't use it as a garnish. For drinks, my rule is that if you would want to taste the flavor of an ingredient in your drink, then you're free to use it as a garnish since drinks are more about flavor infusion than edibility.

Creating an exceptionally well-garnished drink takes attention to detail, time, and skill. Drinks, like food, can become real works of art when they're presented thoughtfully. Garnishes are never a place to skimp; if you're spending good money on quality wine and spirits or other drinks, you want to make sure your garnish matches up.

Making drinks with your creativity, experimentation, bold ideas, and flavors are what will turn you from a drink-maker into a mixologist, and it'll certainly drive up the hype for a fantastic meal. Drinks are kind of like the opening show for a popular band -- they've got to be new and interesting and create some drama for the highlight of the concert.

Whenever I'm trying to create a new drink, I shuffle through my mind for ingredients I haven't used before or think of ways to use classic drink garnishes in new ways. Take for example the citrus peel we mentioned while we discussed old-fashioned drinks. Every bar or home drink-maker will use an orange peel, but what if we took that a cut above and used a *candied* orange peel? When you're trying to come up with ideas, don't be shy about using your online resources.

There are always fresh and daring ideas making it out into the food blogs of the web every day, and it's a great place to learn about new tools and techniques.

Here are some ideas to transform your drink garnishes;

Try using woody-stemmed herbs as your drink skewers. The best ones are rosemary, thyme, sage, and lavender.

Light your garnish on fire—no, seriously. It's a good way to infuse flavor and smokiness into your drink and adds an appealing aroma and a flashy garnish. I would recommend only doing this with hard-stemmed herbs like rosemary, thyme, or lavender and with cinnamon sticks or by putting a hot flame under a citrus peel to drop the oils into the drink and then discarding the peel afterwards. Once the herbs are lit, let them burn for a second and then blow them out right before serving.

Candy your citrus peels and berries. They will be game-changers for your mixed drinks! Candied cranberries and orange peels make the ultimate garnishes for a holiday drink.

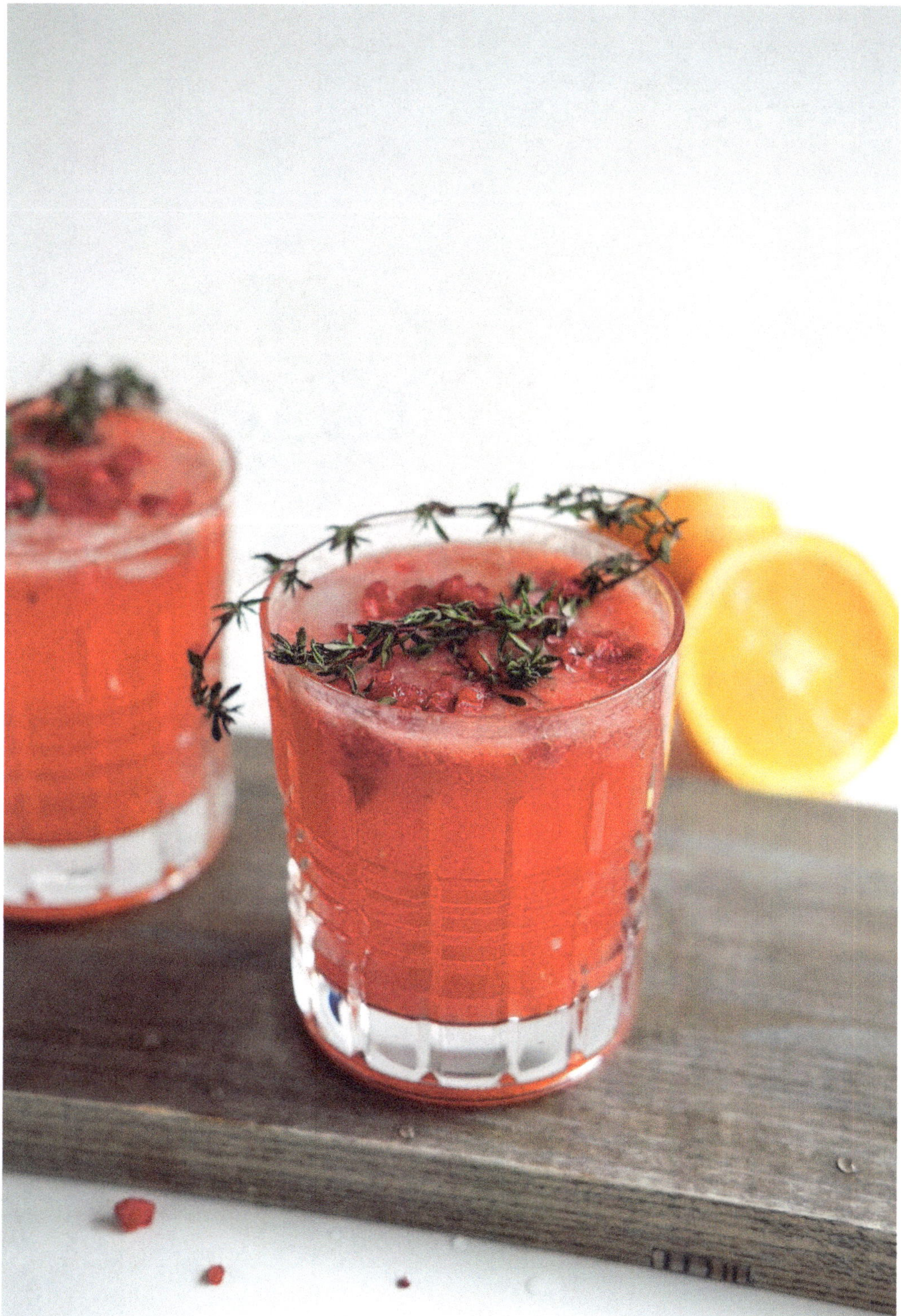

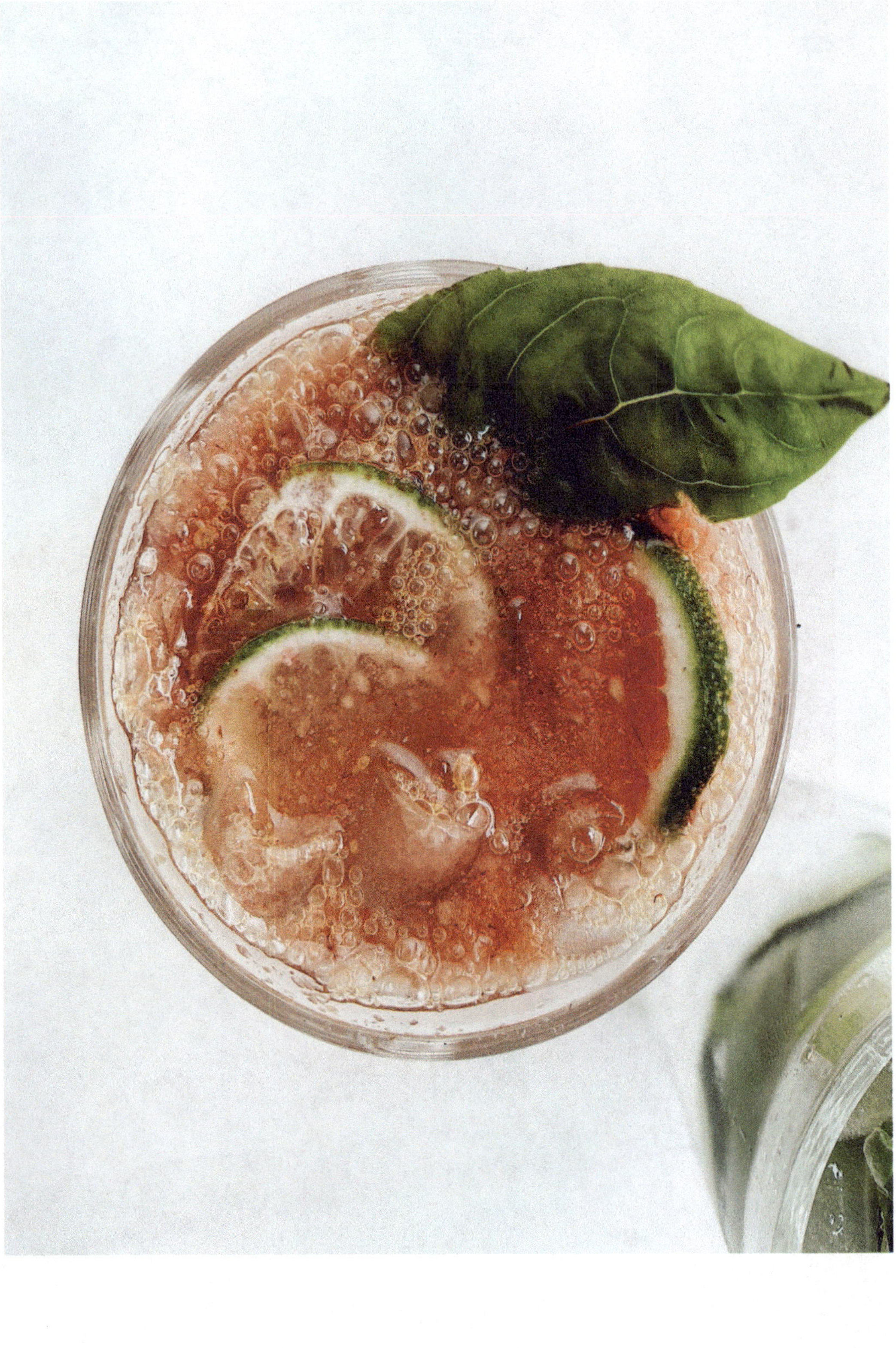

CASE STUDY

(Pictured: pink grapefruit, lime, and basil mojito). Bright & warm flavors from caramelized grapefruit juice, zesty lime, and toasty agave make this the perfect summer cocktail. A simple garnish of a fresh basil leaf adds color and a touch of scent and herbal flavor that balances the acidic grapefruit juice. This is where quality ingredients really shine through -- the fresh garnishes that infuse drinks and catch your eye. Drink garnishes have to be made immediately before serving (the same goes for food, of course, but drinks can have different garnishes that perish more easily). Soft herbs like basil and cilantro or even mint can get muddled and bruised beyond use very easily. They have to be stored appropriately or else they won't be able to stand up to a drink creation. Handle them delicately, buy them fresh, and store them according to their needs.

PINK GRAPEFRUIT & BASIL MOJITO

MAKES: 1 GLASS | TOTAL TIME: 8 MINUTES

INGREDIENTS

2 basil leaves
1 lime wedge
1 shot of rum or vodka
3 lime slices ¼ inch thick
1 tbsp agave
2 medium (or 1 large) grapefruit
Granulated sugar
Sparkling water

DIRECTIONS

Preheat your oven to the broil setting. Slice the grapefruit in half and place onto a foil-lined baking sheet face up. Sprinkle with granulated sugar and broil in the oven for 5 minutes or until the fruit begins to bubble and caramelize, then remove from the oven and allow them to cool.

Cover a small plate with a layer of granulated sugar and use a lime wedge to wet the rim of the glass. Dip the rim onto the plate to coat with sugar and set aside.

Once your grapefruit has cooled, you can start juicing. Using a citrus reamer, juice the grapefruit and strain the pulp and seeds out with a mesh strainer. You should have about ¾ cup of juice. Measure out 1 tbsp of agave and muddle with the lime wedge used to wet the rim and one basil leaf. Add mixture to the juice and stir. Add the shot of vodka or rum along with the lime slices and fill the rest of the glass with sparkling water. Use the last basil leaf as a garnish on top of the drink.

Vegetables

(Pictured: carrot froth on salmon)

Just like fruits, vegetables are so versatile. You can use them in their fresh state for garnishes by peeling, julienning, and mincing. You can also use other cooking techniques like roasting to create garnishes out of vegetables. Foaming a vegetable juice like carrot, celery, or even beet juice can create stunning garnishes. The picture opposite this page showcases a citrus foam on top of a filet of salmon.

Tip: Quick pickling is a great strategy to add brightness and acidity to your dish.

Simply prepare the vegetables to your liking (slicing, julienning, shredding, cut into spears, left whole) and make a solution of seasonings and brine. A brine is composed of equal parts vinegar and water, and any type of vinegar can be used (apple cider, white wine, red wine to name a few).

Keep them in the fridge and try to wait at least 48 hours to let the flavors develop. Check out the quick-pickled red onions recipe on page 101!

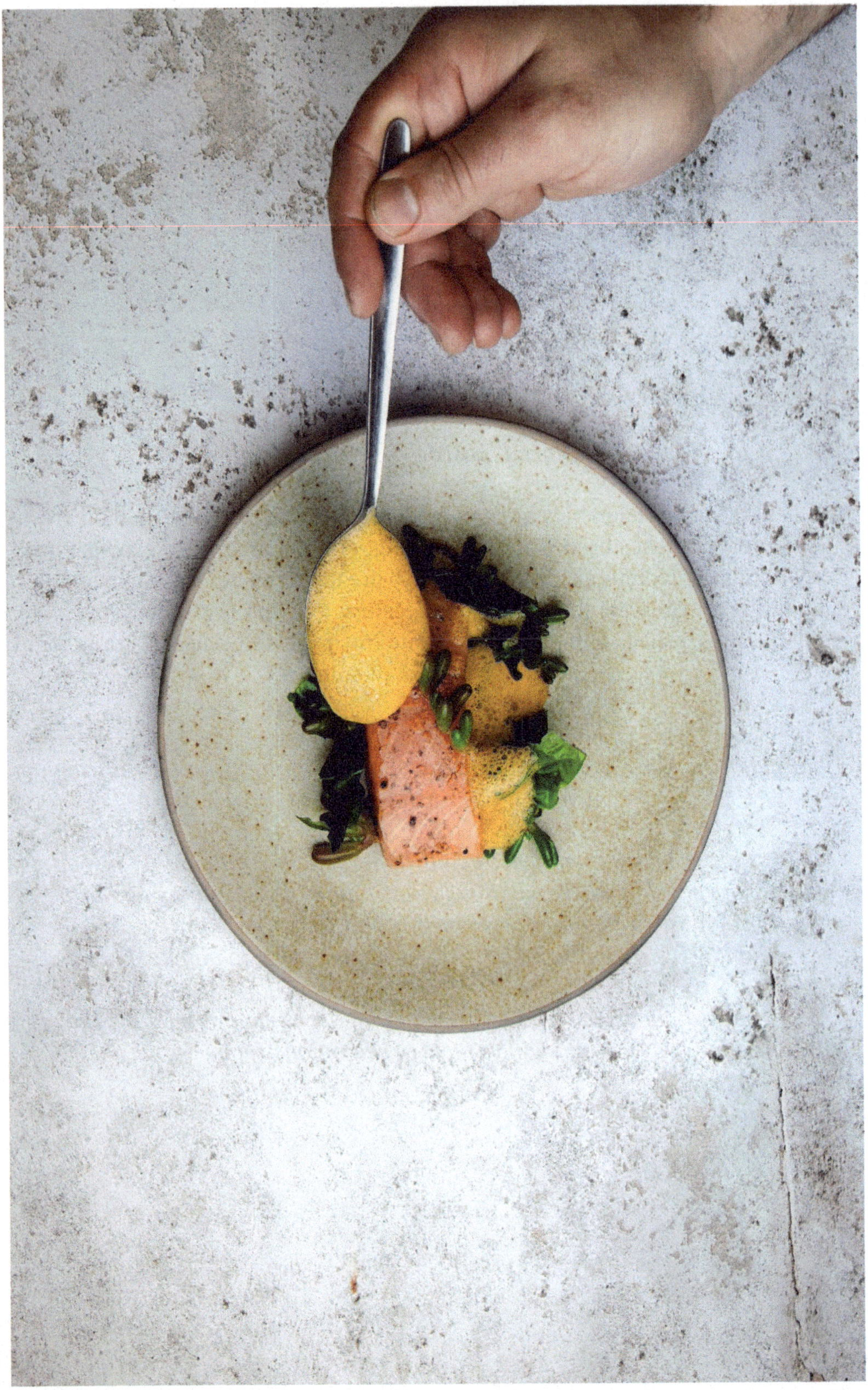

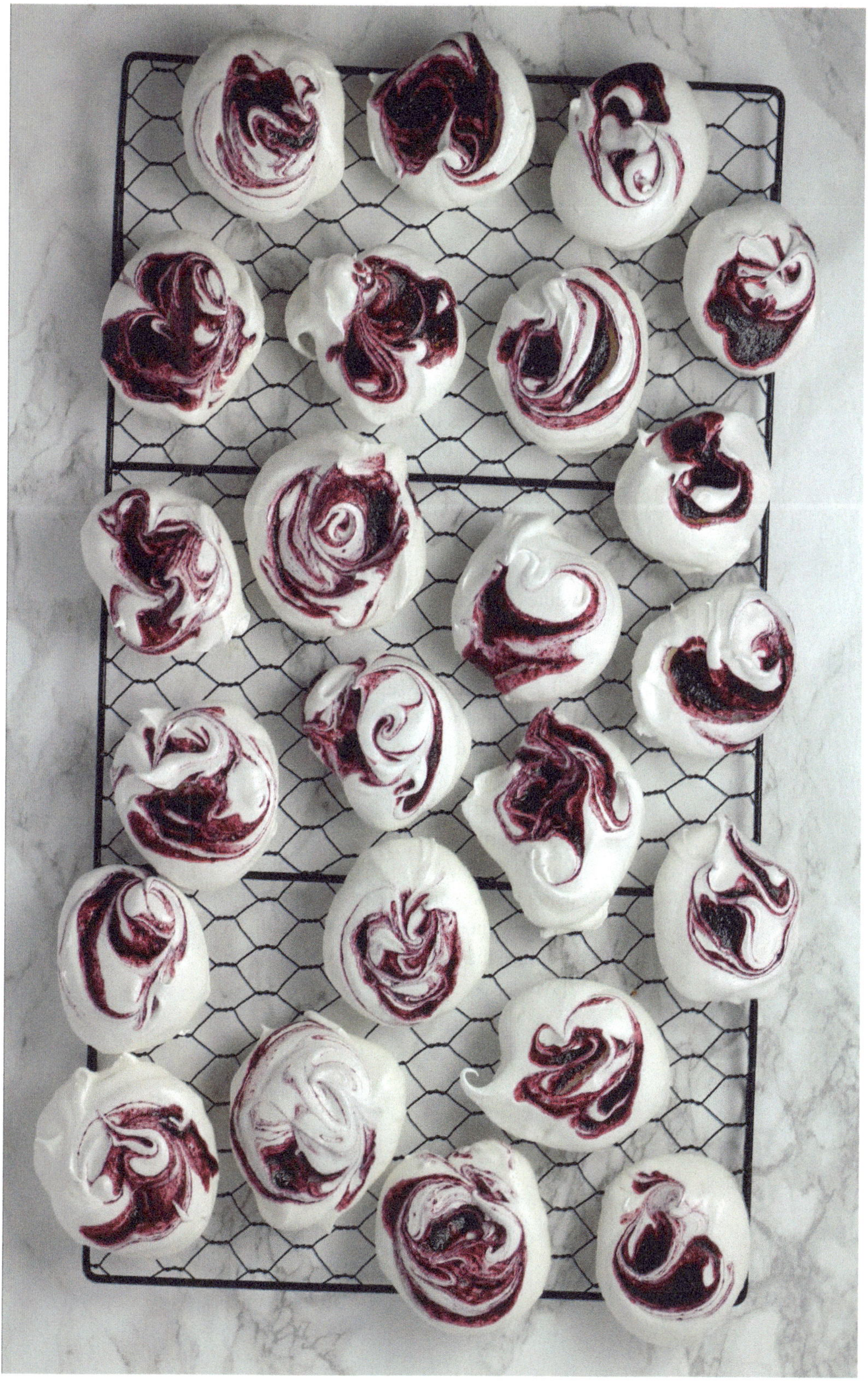

CASE STUDY

(Pictured: meringue cookies with purple swirl). Vegetables don't have to be savory; we know there's carrot cake and sweet potato pie, but there are more opportunities to use vegetables in a unique way. Try combining them with fruits. Imagine a meringue with a beet and blackberry swirl -- earthy flavors combine with the sweetness of a summer blackberry on a puffy egg white cloud. It's sure to grab attention and would even make a show-stopping garnish on top of a cake or other dessert. Vegetables like carrots and beets can also do great as garnishes when they're shaved finely with a zester. They're bright and colorful, and packed with sharp tastes that impact your flavors in huge ways. Also consider using brine and spices to quick-pickle vegetables; doing this will preserve the crunch and layer on big flavors.

Purées

(Pictured: salmon with chimichurri rice, a smoky roasted cauliflower & mushroom purée, and chili oil)

This is where the blender comes in. If you're looking to transform any food, puréeing can be a fantastic way to create a beautiful garnish that's full of color and flavor. You can also add in spices or seasonings to enhance flavors and use a spoon or utensil to garnish onto a plate. Voila! Dish upgraded.

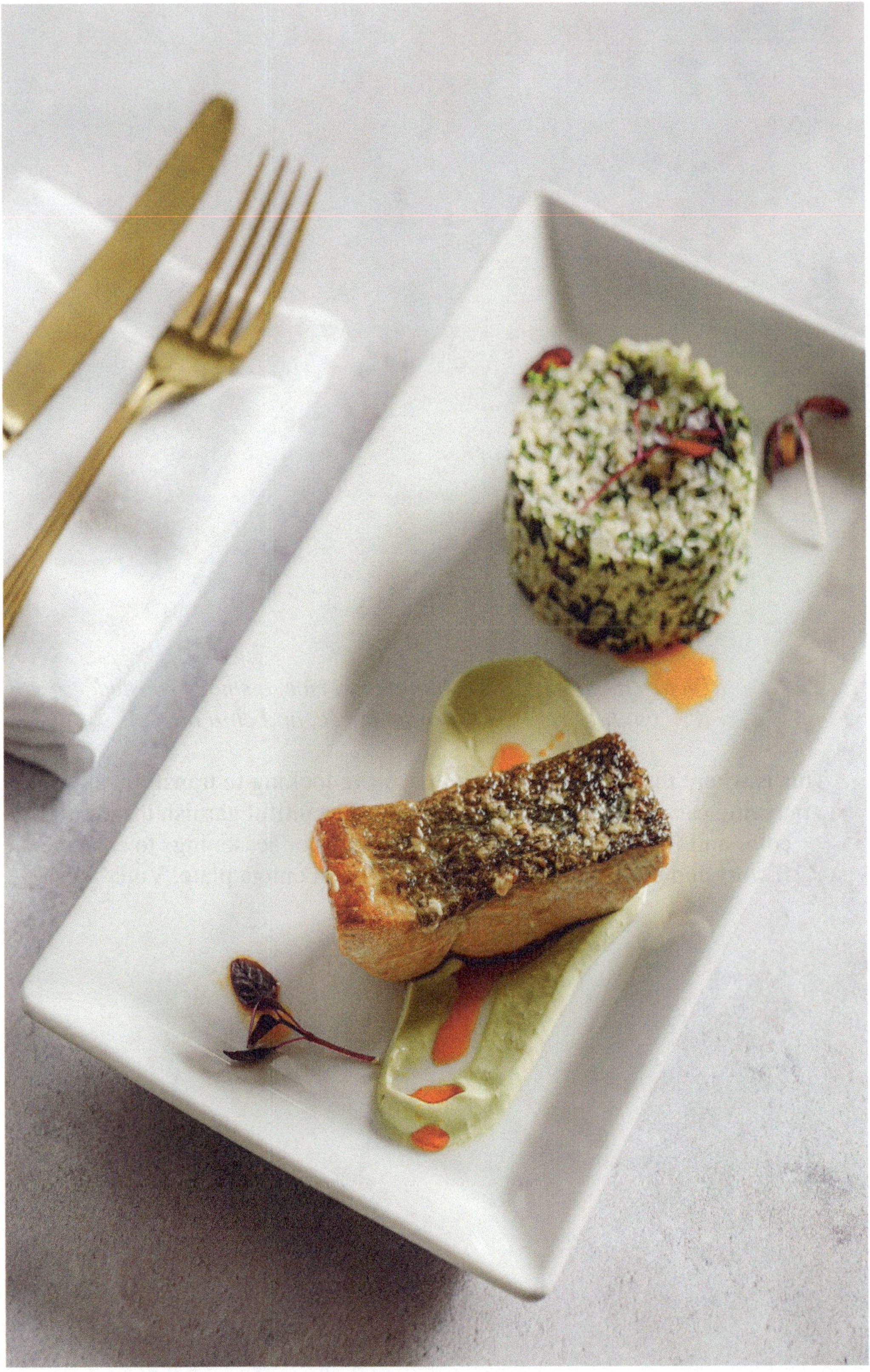

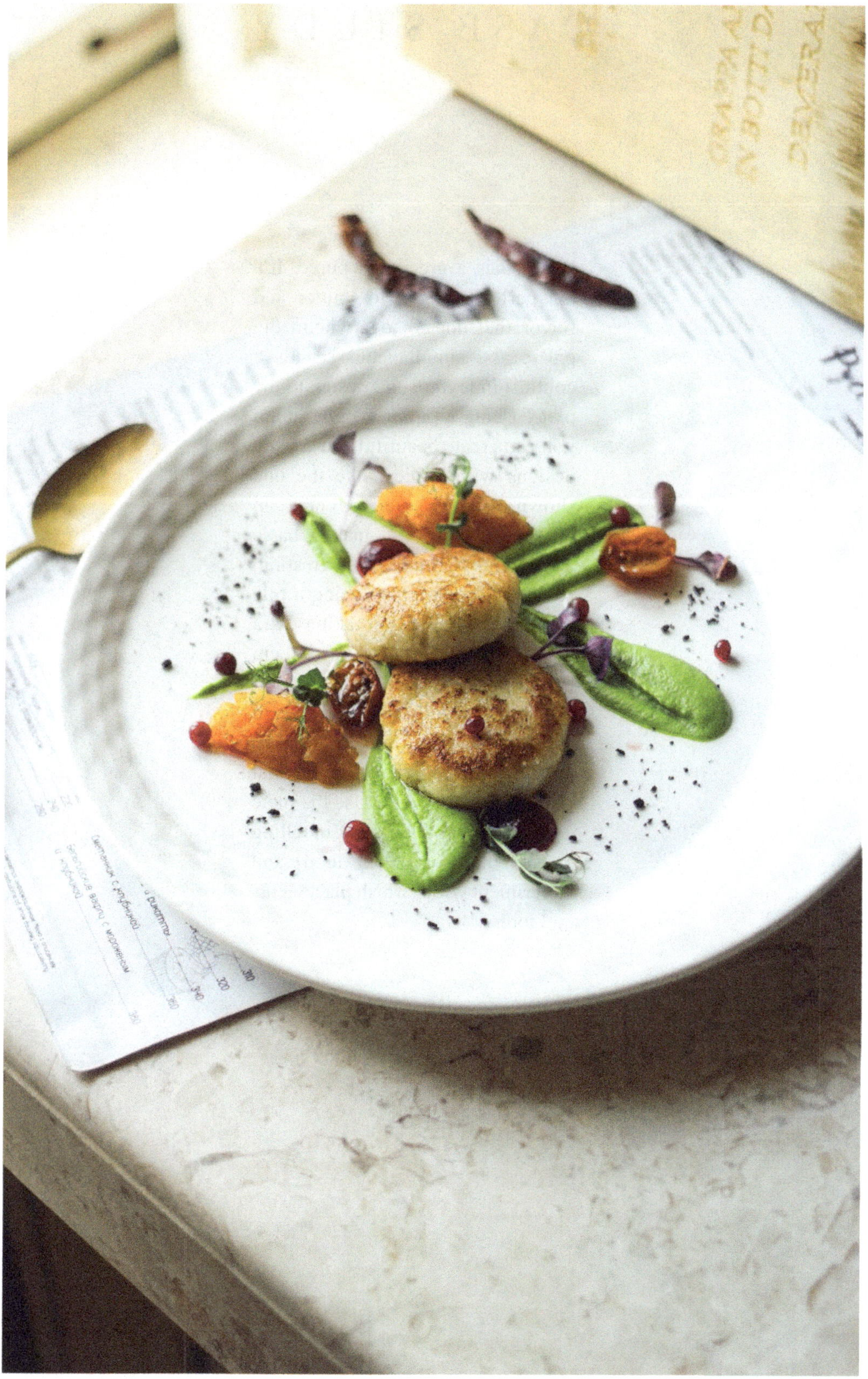

CASE STUDY

Pictured is a green pea purée. It's the perfect vehicle for butter and flavor that doesn't overwhelm the palate and simultaneously adds a contrast in texture and design to the plate. Using a piping bag or spoon you can create beautiful and artistic designs with purées, like the one shown above. Purées are an excellent way to make basic ingredients more interesting. Everybody is used to seeing a pile of peas on a plate, but taking extra time to really incorporate them creatively draws attention to it. It transforms a simple dinner like crab cakes and peas into a modern delicacy and artistic statement that guests will gush over. Use the plate as your playground (yes, I'm telling you to play with your food) and experiment with garnish placements and tools.

SIMPLE PURÉE

PREP TIME: 5 MINUTES

DIRECTIONS

Any food can be puréed using a blender or food processor.

Start by cooking the ingredient until it's completely soft (a fork goes through easily), toss into the blender, pour in just enough heavy cream or dairy alternative to get the blender blades turning easily, then add a few tablespoons of cold butter (never sub in melted or soft) and blend until smooth.

Tip: I've found that cooling down the emulsion in a metal bowl on top of an ice bath is a great way to ensure that the purée sets nicely.

Drizzles: Glazes, Sauces, and Syrups

(Pictured: salted caramel drizzle)

Nobody can deny the appeal of a good drizzle. Sweet, salty, creamy, and dribbled onto food to perfection. This is where your inner artist really gets to shine. You can drizzle with a spoon, chopstick, brush, or even a butter knife.

If you're looking for precision and perfect lines, try using a pastry bag (or a plain old plastic sandwich bag with the end cut off) to decorate.

Tip: You want to be quick with your drizzling to prevent lumpy or uneven lines.

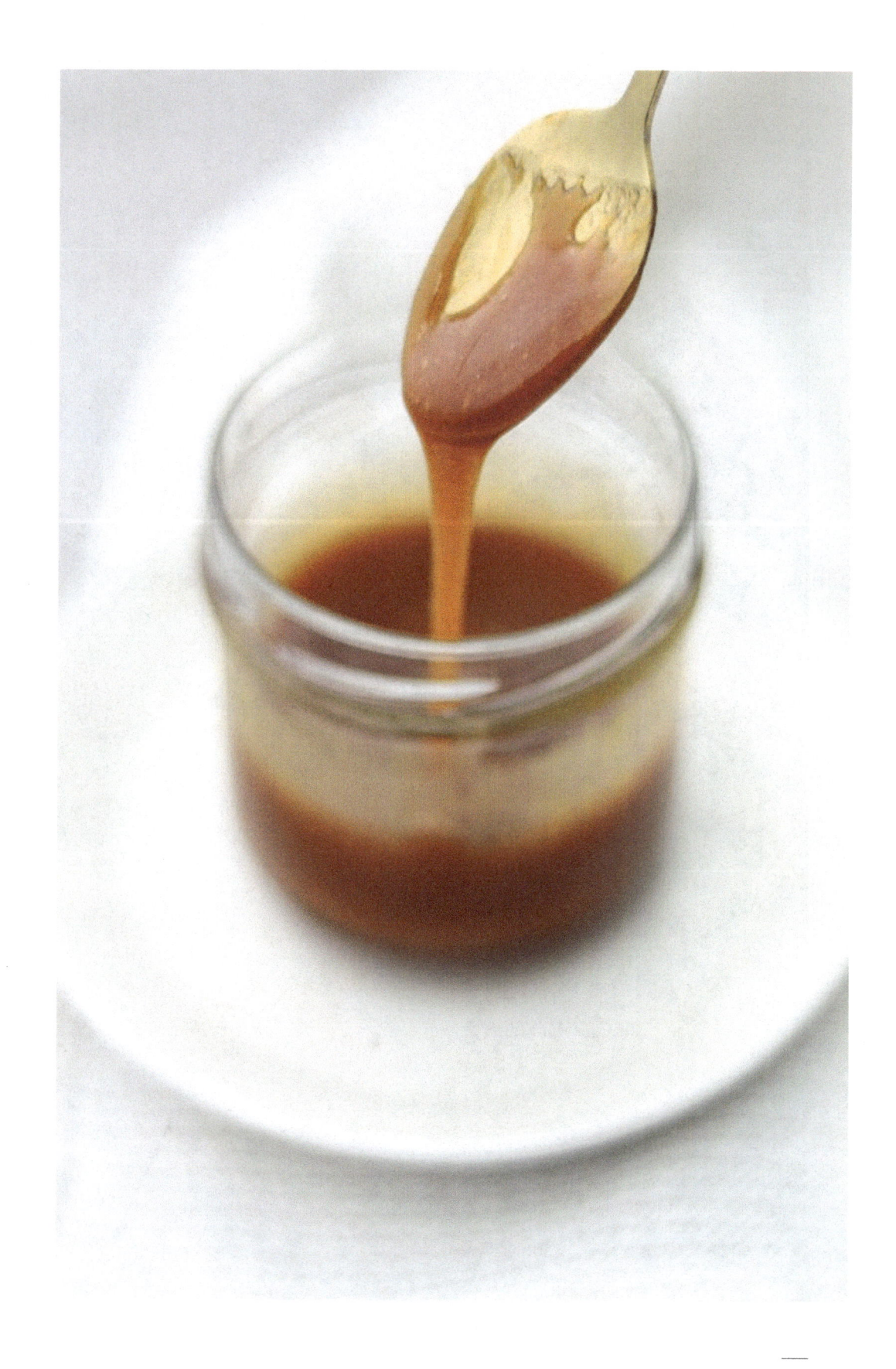

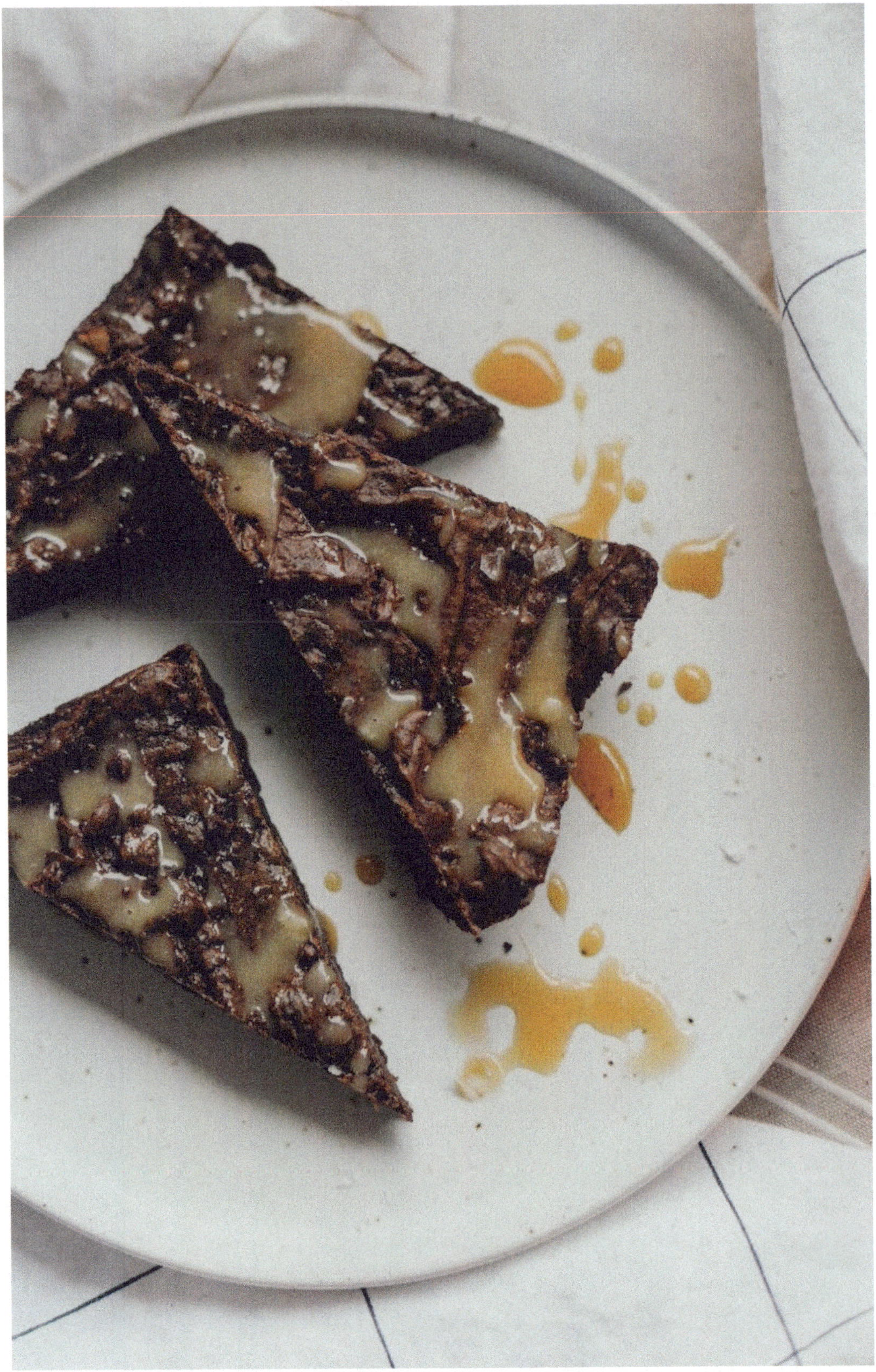

CASE STUDY

(Pictured: brownie with caramel drizzle). The caramel drizzle -- famously incredible on ice cream and frappes, and basically anything sweet and delicious you could possibly stick a name to. Let's talk about being messy for a second. As you'll notice about this plate, the caramel drizzle on top isn't laid out in perfectly neat lines or designs; it's poured loosely straight on top and it's nothing short of a little messy and asymmetrical. But that's kind of the beauty of it: designs don't have to be linear to be perfect. You'll notice that the brownie is cut into wedges, which is untypical. It's also stacked neatly on top of another wedge, with another piece positioned next to it. This uneven positioning makes it look more artistic and sophisticated.

Toppings

(Pictured: pizza with toppings)

Who doesn't love toppings? I'm that person at the froyo bar with more toppings than yogurt. Toppings are always an easy way to add color and pops of flavor to your dish. They're perfect garnishes because they're functional, visually attractive, and pack on flavor. Crackers on soup, fried shallots on a salad, chocolate chips on pancakes, and pepperoni on pizza are all toppings we know and love.

Tip: Try roasting nuts and seeds on a cast iron pan with seasonings. My favorite garnish for pesto pasta is toasted pine nuts -- it's a must-try. You can also toast legumes like chickpeas to give them crunch and flavor and turn them into perfect garnishing toppings.

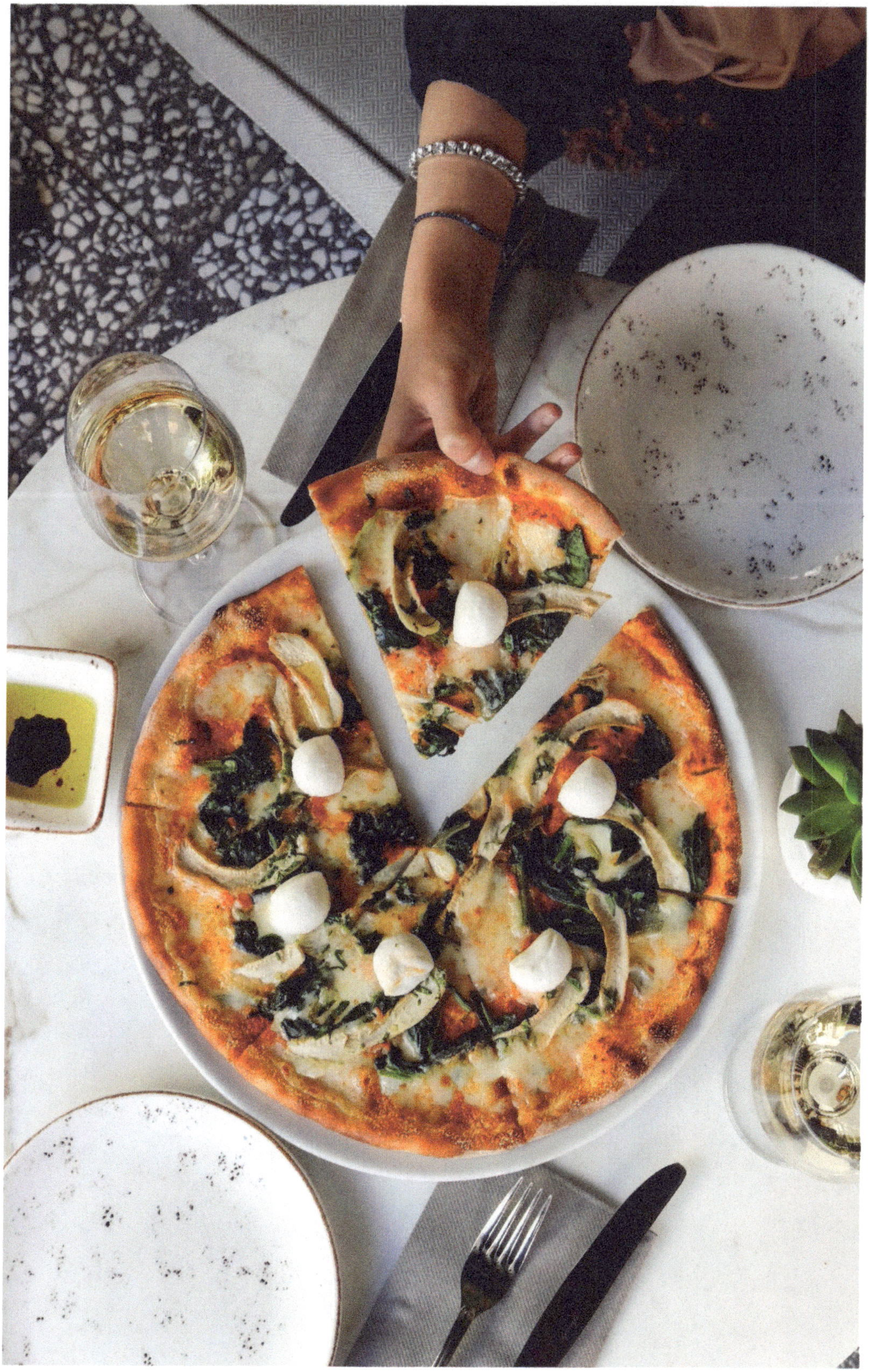

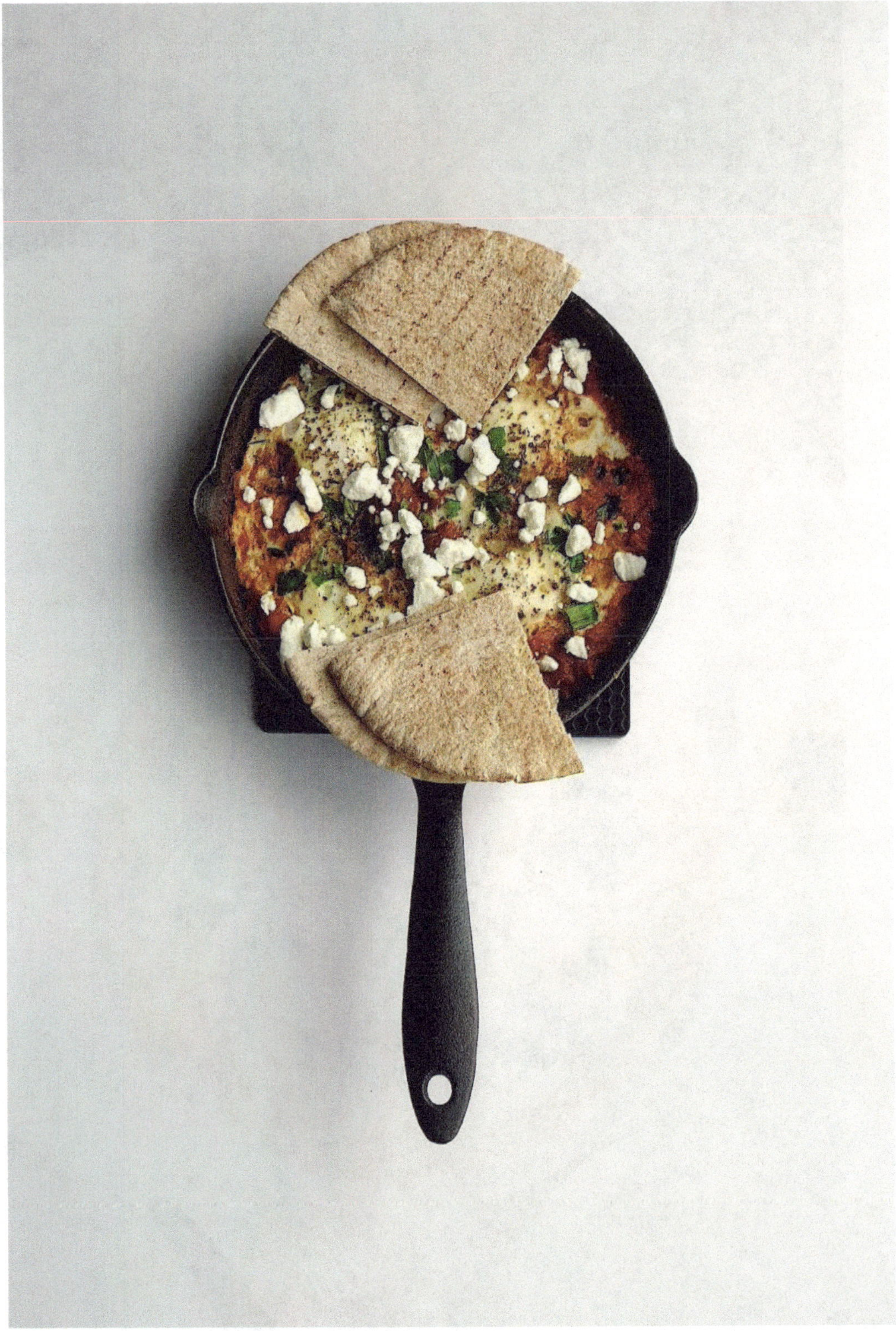

CASE STUDY

(Pictured: Shakshuka with feta, herbs, and pita bread). Let's talk about this skillet -- why does it work as a serving plate? Well for starters, anybody who has a cast iron pan knows it keeps things hot for a long time. This works great in a restaurant or dining setting where people might be talking or serving for awhile and you'll want to keep things hot for longer. The cast iron as a plate is a novelty experience for guests and is a great platter for shareable dishes like this shakshuka, pasta, or a paella. Picking a plate that addresses the way the dish will be eaten is important too. For dishes like this, that need to finish cooking in the oven or need something with sides, this cast iron pan works great. Toppings as garnishes work well to add a variety of flavors, textures, and colors to the plate. The toppings of feta and cilantro pictured here add a much-needed brightness both visually and flavor-wise to the spicy red pepper sauce and eggs.

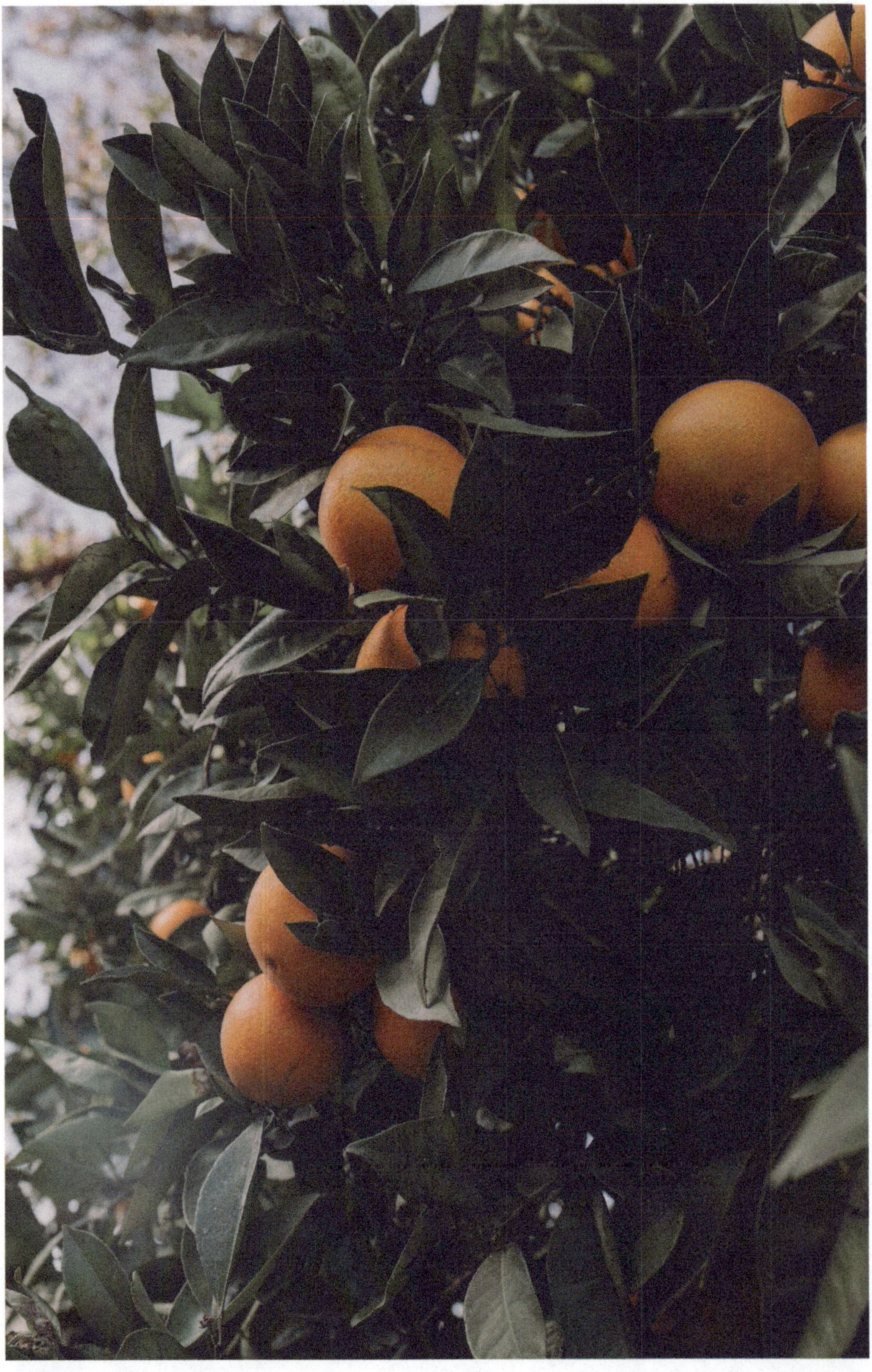

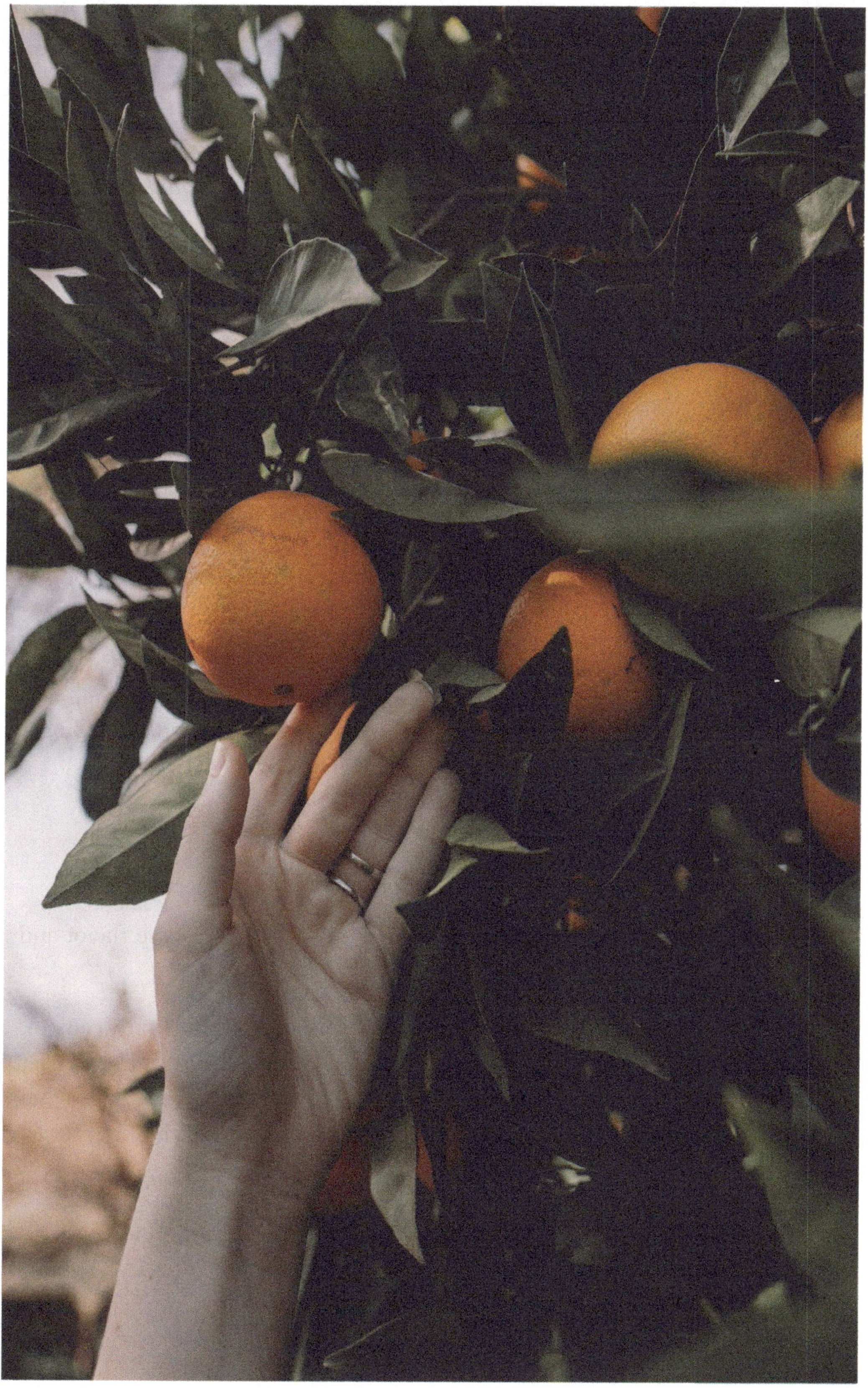

GATHERING INGREDIENTS

The key to fantastic garnishes is using fresh ingredients. Fresher means better texture, flavor, and color. If you want to go one step further, make sure to choose quality ingredients too. In this instance, quality means buying as close to the ground as possible -- think farmer's market, your local co-operative, your own garden.

If you don't have access to those, it's okay! Just focus on sourcing your ingredients as fresh as you can possibly get them.

Buying Ingredients

While you're shopping, if you're unfamiliar with an ingredient and how to use it, check with the grower or stocker and ask them about it. They can tell you how to prepare it, tell when it's ripe, and determine what the flavor should be and what it pairs well with.

You can also do a quick search on the internet and you should find all the information you need. It'll also simplify things for you in the long run if you go into your shopping experience with a list and an idea of the dish you want to make.

Storing Ingredients

If you purchase garnish ingredients a couple of days to a week ahead of time, it's important to keep them as fresh as possible to preserve flavor and color. To do that, be sure you're storing your ingredients correctly.

1. **Check the fridge temperature if it's an ingredient that needs to be kept cold.** If the temperature is too cold for soft fruit like berries for example, they'll freeze and when they thaw out, they'll lose their structure. This can make it tough to garnish if you're looking for a plump berry shape.

    Another tip for berries is to store them in a flat layer on top of a paper towel rather than on top of each other. They'll last longer and you'll reduce the risk of your berries getting moldy or being crushed.

2. **If you've got fresh leafy herbs you won't be using right away, trim the ends of the stems off**, place in a jar filled with water, cover leaves with a plastic bag and place in the fridge. Woody stemmed herbs do better wrapped in a damp paper towel inside an airtight container.

3. **If you're storing anything in the freezer, make sure it's safe from freezer burn.** To do this, double wrap with wax paper or aluminum foil and stuff inside a resealable bag or invest in durable reusable bags.

4. **Dehydrate herbs, fruits, and flowers.** They can be saved for decorations or spice mixtures.

5. **Freeze ingredients into ice cubes.** Fruit, herbs, and leftover juices frozen into ice cubes make flavorful additions to drinks.

Repurpose Your Tidbits for Garnishes

No matter what you're making, there will almost always be tidbits leftover from the cooking process. One of my greatest challenges is finding out what to do with those things. Luckily there are plenty of recipes out there just for that reason, and a lot of those ends and pieces can be used to make new garnishes too.

As you're creating your dish, you're likely to have some extra ingredients leftover, especially once you've plated your food. Entirely new elements can be made for your dish or to future ones using these. Your objective is to transform them into something useful. Leftover bread can become flavored breadcrumbs, berries that go soft can be made into jelly or jam, and citrus and herbs can be frozen into ice cubes.

Here are some of my favorite ways to repurpose ingredients for new garnishes:

> *Candied citrus peels or leaves*
>
> *Make oleo saccharum (sweet citrus oil syrup) from peels*
>
> *Fruit, flowers, and leaves frozen into ice cubes*

Breadcrumbs or breadcrumb 'sand' to add interesting texture (can also be done using cookies or baked goods or graham crackers)

Purées

Infusions from peels, stems, and leaves

Fruit leather from juiced fruit pulp

Create flavored sugar for drink rims using citrus peels or dried flowers

Below is a list of some of my favorite garnishing ingredients to get you started.

GARNISH INGREDIENTS

- Herbs (fresh and dried)
- Cocoa powder
- Powdered sugar
- Berries
- Salt
- Seasonings
- Olive oil (the good stuff)
- Limes and lemons
- Seeds (sesame, pomegranate, etc)
- Honey
- Candied peels and leaves
- Microgreens and sprouts
- Pickled onions (or anything pickled)
- Capers
- Avocado
- Fried shallots

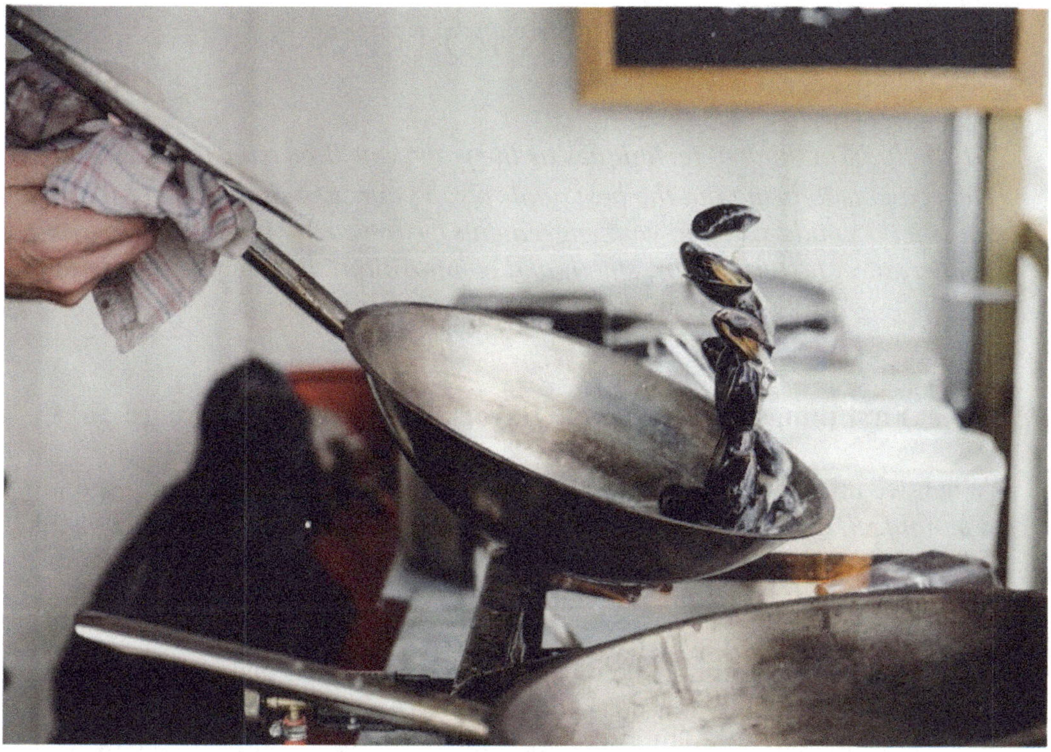

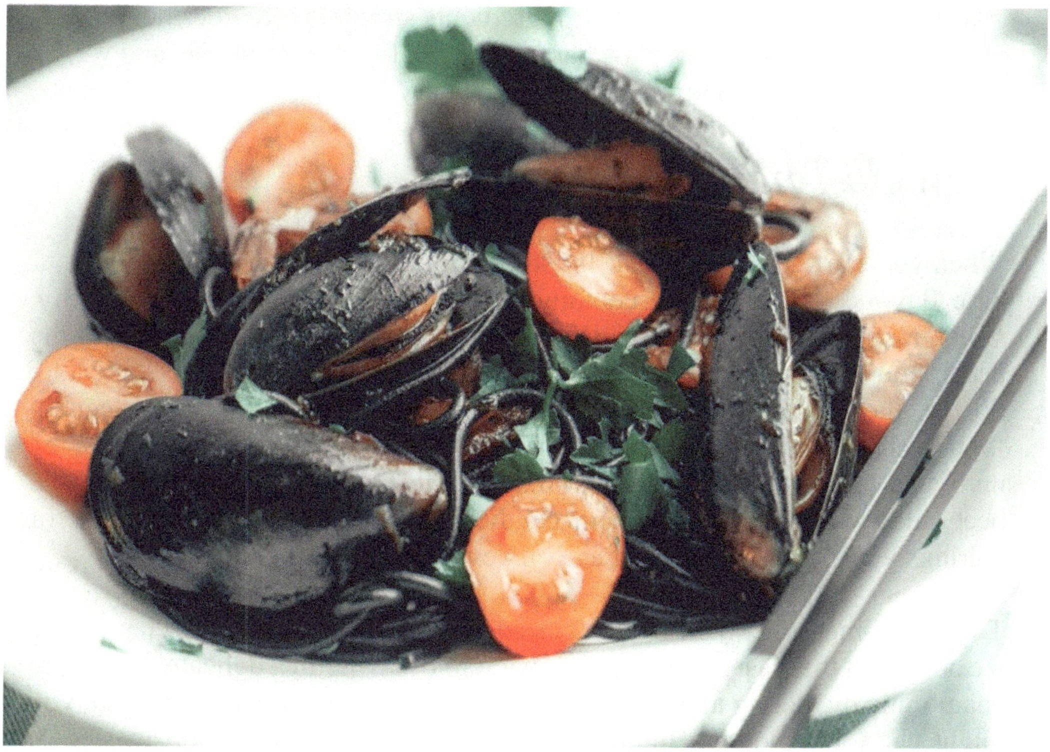

TECHNIQUES

It's helpful to think of techniques as the ways you'll be transforming your ingredients to bring out the best qualities in your dish and garnish. What can you do to add value to your ingredients? How can you add variety using temperature, texture, color, smell, and composition? Before we get into the nitty-gritty, we have to cover some flavor basics.

First things first; taste and flavor are two different things.

When we taste, our senses naturally search for depth in flavor and respond to *mouthfeel,* the physical sensations in the mouth created by a food. Taste is what the tongue reports to the brain. Taste is made up of sweet, sour, salty, bitter, umami, and fat. Flavor comes from smell.

Aromatic compounds are chemical compounds in food that create aromas that are interpreted by our nose and brain. The more aromatic compounds foods have in common with each other, the more likely they are to pair well together. That's why things like chocolate and bacon go well together. As you're cooking, try to keep your ingredients simple; more does not equal better. Think of the tastes and characteristics of your ingredients and work on creating complementary flavors.

How do I pair flavors?

When you start garnishing, you'll want to think of what pairs well with your base flavors. Say you were cooking beets; you'd describe them as earthy, sweet, maybe a little spicy. In this case, nuts compliment the earthiness of the beets, and if you candy or glaze them, they'll build on the sweetness too. Spices like cinnamon also go well with beets. Dairy products, especially fermented ones like cheese and yogurt, will add brightness and contrast to the nutty and earthy flavors. The final dish might look like a cinnamon-roasted beet salad with goat cheese and candied pecans. These are the types of pairings you'll want to think of as you develop your garnishing skills.

There are times when you'll want a milder flavor, such as making chamomile ice cream. In this case, you wouldn't want to overwhelm a delicate flavor like chamomile by adding a rich, dark chocolate drizzle as a garnish. Instead, you might choose something lighter like a salted caramel drizzle or a piece of honeycomb.

What is plate composition?

Plate composition is the presentation of the elements of the dish. These elements include the *main item,* the *side or supporting elements, sauces,* and the *garnish.*
A great dish balances textures, colors, and flavors. You'll know you've created something with good composition when you get excited to photograph it. Like a fantastic art piece, it'll be something you want to remember. Keep in mind, the best garnishes are simple and complement the other flavors of the dish. If you're plating your food tastefully, you shouldn't need to make up for anything by using flashy garnishes like cucumber flowers or crazy fruit carvings. In other words, garnishes are there to add something meaningful. Learning to plate well takes practice until you can develop an intuition and taste for it. It will require you to be judicious on each plating occasion to decide what will best enhance your creation. In the end, what matters most is that you're proud to serve whatever you create.

What makes a garnish palatable?

Palatable garnishes are those which are not only edible but are also properly incorporated into the dish itself. A great garnish is one that echoes the flavors of your dish and works to enhance it. Garnishes should never be about adding color or simply for looks; they should be a part of the dish.

Example: a dusting of matcha powder on top of a matcha flavored dessert.

How do techniques transform ingredients?

Ingredients can be transformed through temperature, spices, seasonings, pickling, curing, fermentation, drying, marination, reduction, and infusion. Each technique brings out different flavors and qualities.
To create a good garnish, take an ingredient from an element of the dish and use a technique to capture a different variation of the same flavor.

Example: Use a preserved lemon slice to garnish baked salmon. The process of spicing and preserving lemons in oil makes the rind edible and adds citrus flavor to the oil. Leftover oil can be used to drizzle over the salmon as a garnish or even be used to create a dressing for a side salad.

How do I create contrast?

Creating contrast in your dish draws in both the eyes and taste buds. Visually, we look for contrast to draw our attention, so your goal in composing your dish should be the same. The brightness and color of the food will heighten this, as well as a variety of textures and shapes. Before food reaches the mouth, our brain relies on smell to indicate flavor. Garnishes can help to create contrast in smell to add an appetizing appeal.

Example: Think of a squeeze of a lemon or the aroma of spicy arugula on a prosciutto pizza.

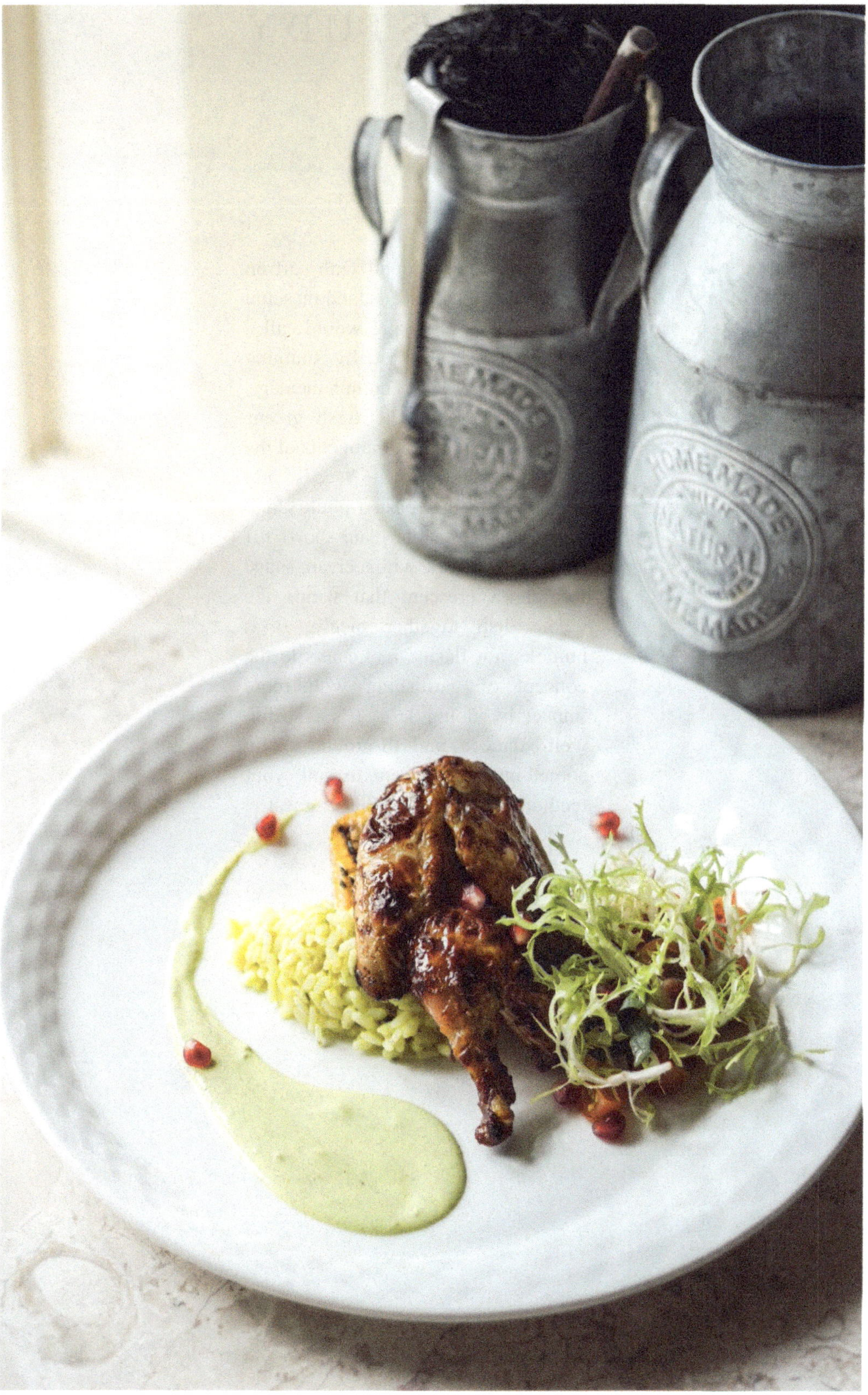
HOME MADE
NATURAL

CASE STUDY

(Pictured: roasted quail with saffron rice, pomegranate seeds, and mesclun greens). This is what I would call a perfect plate. It's visually stunning and its flavors are complementary. The crispiness of the fresh greens contrasts the softer components of the dish and pomegranate seeds add brightness to the roasted poultry and savory rice. A white plate shows off the display nicely, with a cream sauce forming a crescent that wraps the whole dish together nicely. It is humble, not flashy, and caters to the concept of garnishing with more impact by doing less. It's colorful, well-balanced, and all around totally something you'd want to sink your teeth into or serve to a dinner guest.

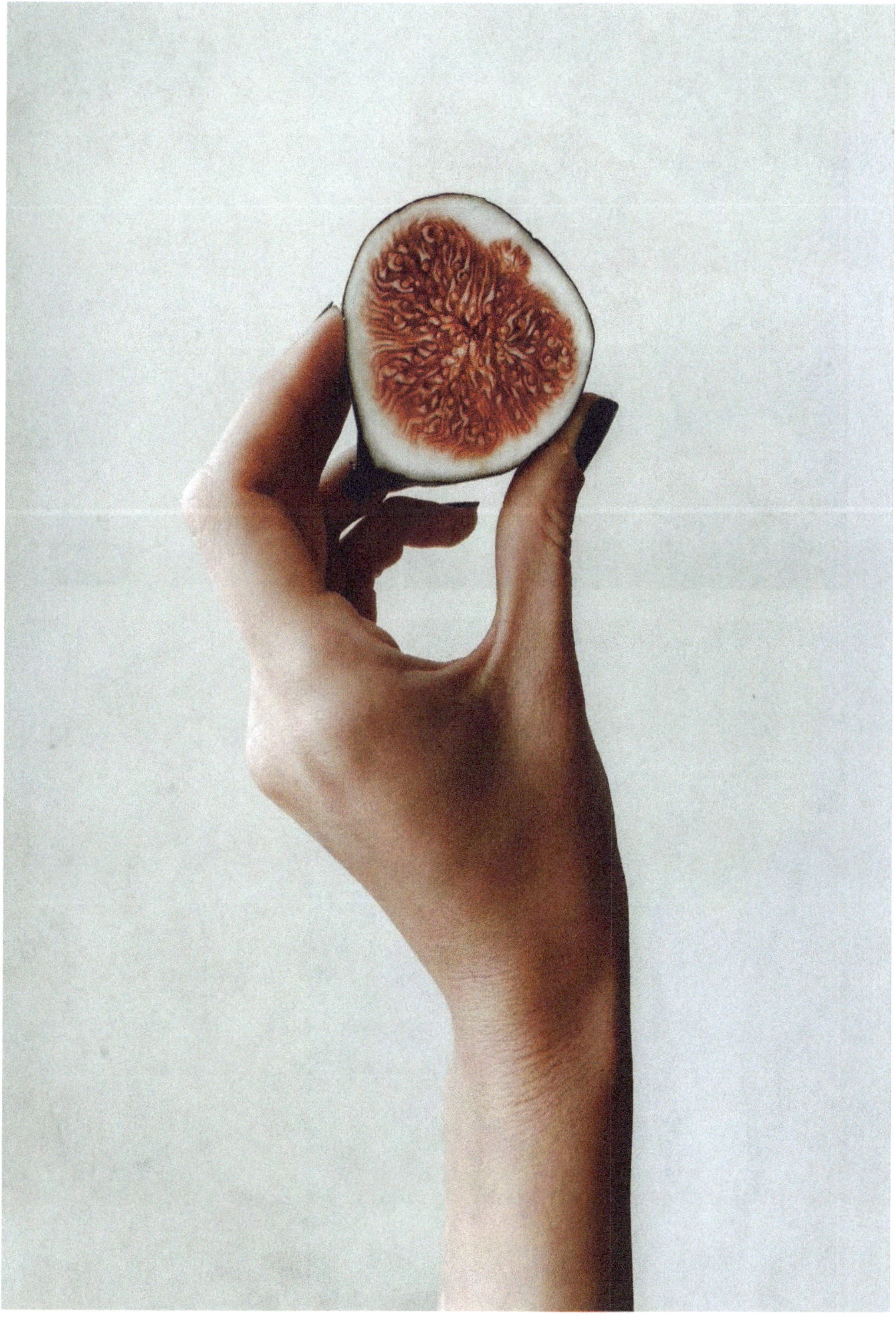

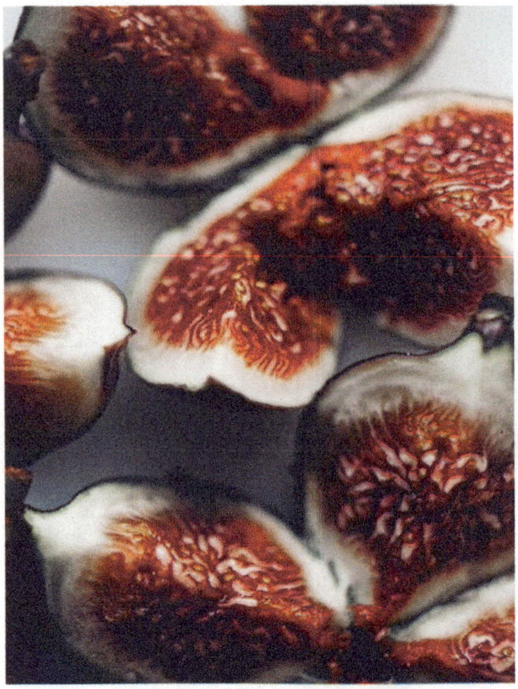
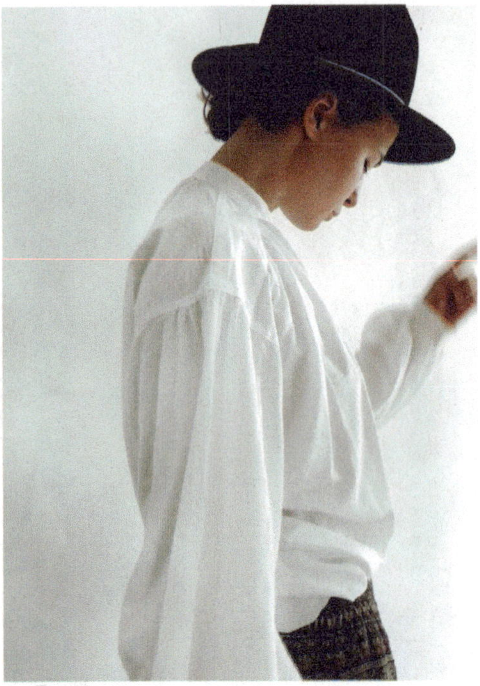
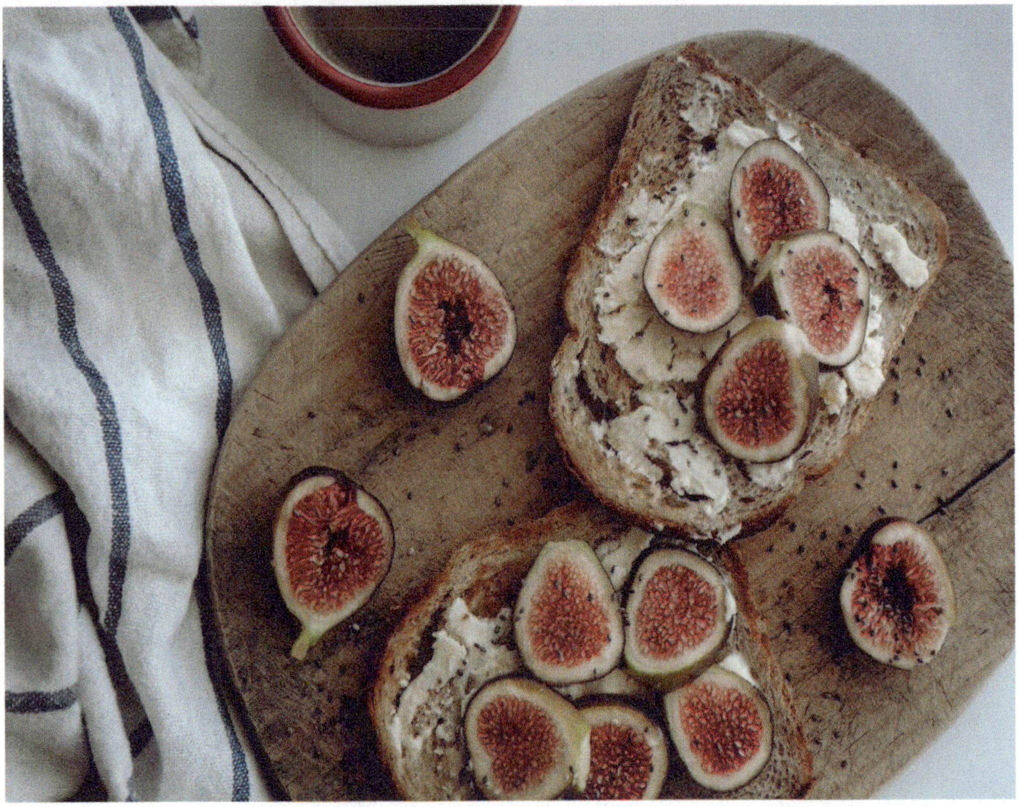

PAIRING FLAVORS & TEXTURES

At every party there is always at least one bowl of chips and dip. Why? Because they're perfect together. Crispy and creamy go together like PB & J. Once you understand the principles of texture and flavor pairings, you'll be whipping up matches made in heaven just like that.

Have you ever heard of palate fatigue? It's basically when your taste buds and nose become overworked from tasting things. If you've ever shopped for perfume or cologne, you've probably seen or perhaps even used the bowls filled with coffee beans. Those are there to serve as a sort of 'palate cleanser' so that your brain can start to distinguish different smells again. In the same sense, you want to ensure that your dish won't tire out taste buds after a few spoonfuls.

One bite of a sweet cake might be fine but if you make it too sweet, a whole slice could be too much. This is why it's so important to taste as you go and to choose garnishes that offer a break from other textures and flavors. Also take into consideration the other elements of the dish. If you're making something spicy, try to add something to the plate that's creamy or sour (or both) and plainer in taste. It's okay to make things that are strong in flavor as long as they contrast with something completely different. You've got to keep things stimulating for the palate, so it doesn't lose interest.

Unlikely pairings are going to be your secret weapon. Just like videos of tigers cuddling bunnies go viral, so do strange flavor pairings. Think of strawberries and balsamic, ice cream and french fries, cheese and apples, chili and watermelon, grapefruit and basil, chocolate and bacon. They're weird but they work in a can't-put-your-finger-on-it type of way. I'm not saying you have to come up with something strange and unusual, but don't be afraid to experiment.

Textures also have their own unusual counterparts. That's why people put oyster crackers on their chowder, granola on yogurt, croutons on a salad, or toppings on their froyo. They're all garnishes and they serve to create contrast and interest in food. When you're craving a food or snack it's usually because you're craving a specific texture just as much as you are a flavor. You'll crave a bag of chips for the crunch just as much as you will for the salt.

There are five types of food textures: *watery (think of soup), creamy (yogurt, mousse, purees), crispy (chips)*, *crunchy (granola)*, *chewy (bread, grains), and firm/hard (vegetables, fruits)*. If prepared and paired with other textures the right way, all textures can go together, but there are some easy matches for textures that are sure to be great combinations. Like textures, all tastes also have the ability to pair well with each other if they're balanced correctly. There are six types of tastes: *sweet (think of honey, sugar or maple syrup), sour (like lemons or vinegar), salty (salt, seafood), bitter (green tea, dandelion greens),* and *umami (miso, meats, cheeses, mushrooms)*.

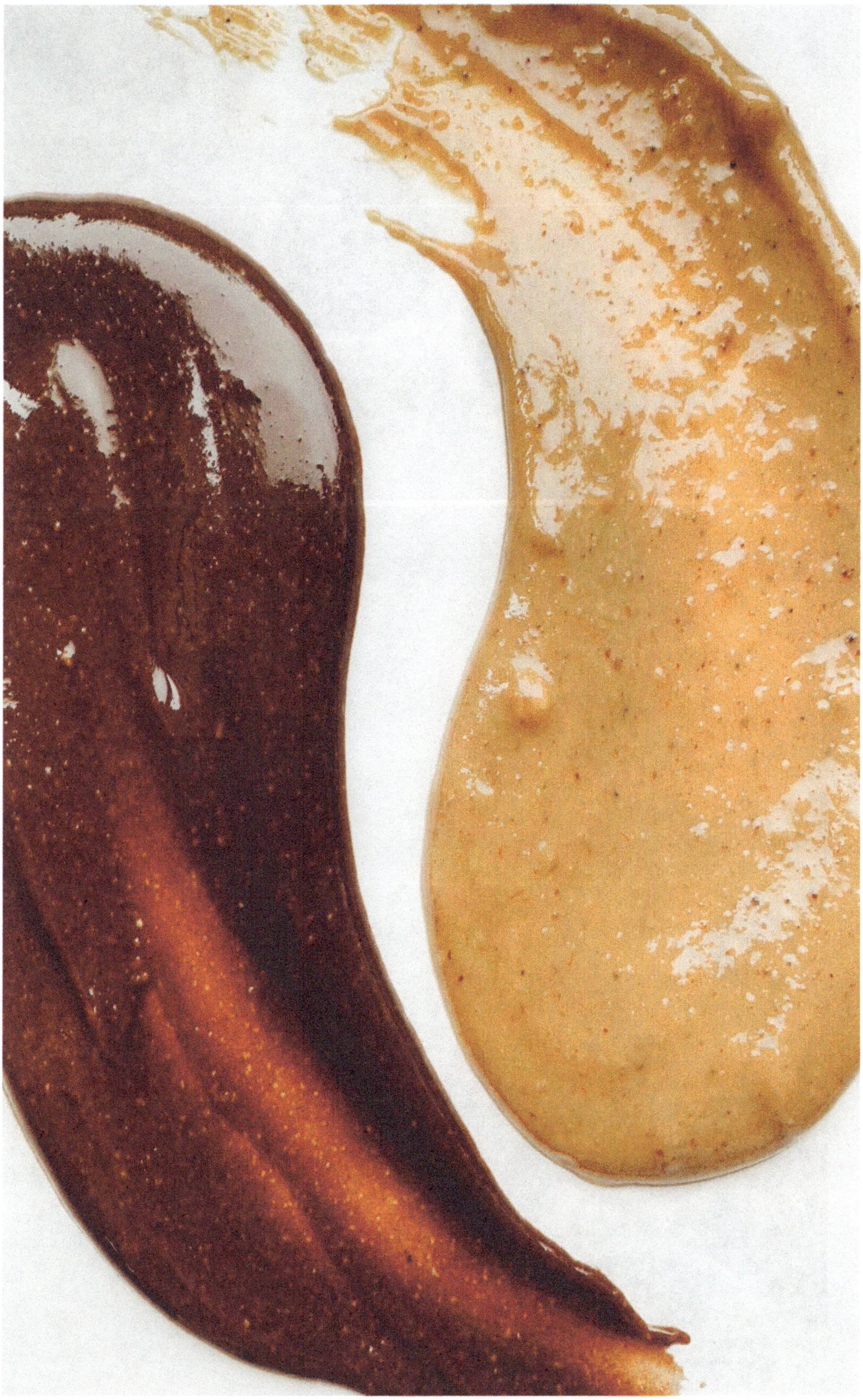

82

TEXTURES PAIRINGS

Watery (broths, soups, liquids)	*Chewy, Crunchy, Firm/Hard*
Creamy (yogurt, mousse, purees)	*Chewy, Crunchy, Crispy, Firm/Hard*
Crispy (chips, fried shallots).	*Chewy, Creamy, Firm/Hard*
Crunchy (croutons, granola)	*Watery, Creamy, Firm/Hard*
Chewy (bread, grains, pasta, meats, shellfish)	*Crispy, Watery, Creamy, Firm/Hard*
Firm/hard (vegetables, fruits)	*All Textures*

TASTES PAIRINGS

Sweet (honey, sugar, maple syrup)	*All Tastes*
Sour (citrus, vinegar, fermented foods)	*All Tastes*
Salty (salt, seafood)	*All Tastes*
Bitter (green tea, cranberries, dandelion greens)	*All Tastes*
Umami (miso, seaweed, aged cheeses, seafood, mushrooms)	*All Tastes*
Fat (butter, cream, oil)	*All Tastes*

The secret here is ratios. As you'll notice with taste pairing, all tastes have the potential to pair well with any other taste. The key is to find the balance of those two tastes or textures to create something harmonious. For example, most wouldn't describe a chocolate chip cookie as salty, and yet the smallest amount of salt can truly take the cookie's flavor to the next level.

The same thing goes for any other taste; chocolate is awakened by coffee, butter marries the intense sweetness of caramel, sour cream or citrus cuts a spicy dish. My best advice is to always taste what you're making, constantly. Flavors are continuously being changed and developed as time goes by, so the best way to ensure a great dish is by tasting as you go. As you prepare to plate your creation, be sure to keep in mind the ratios of the dish's components.

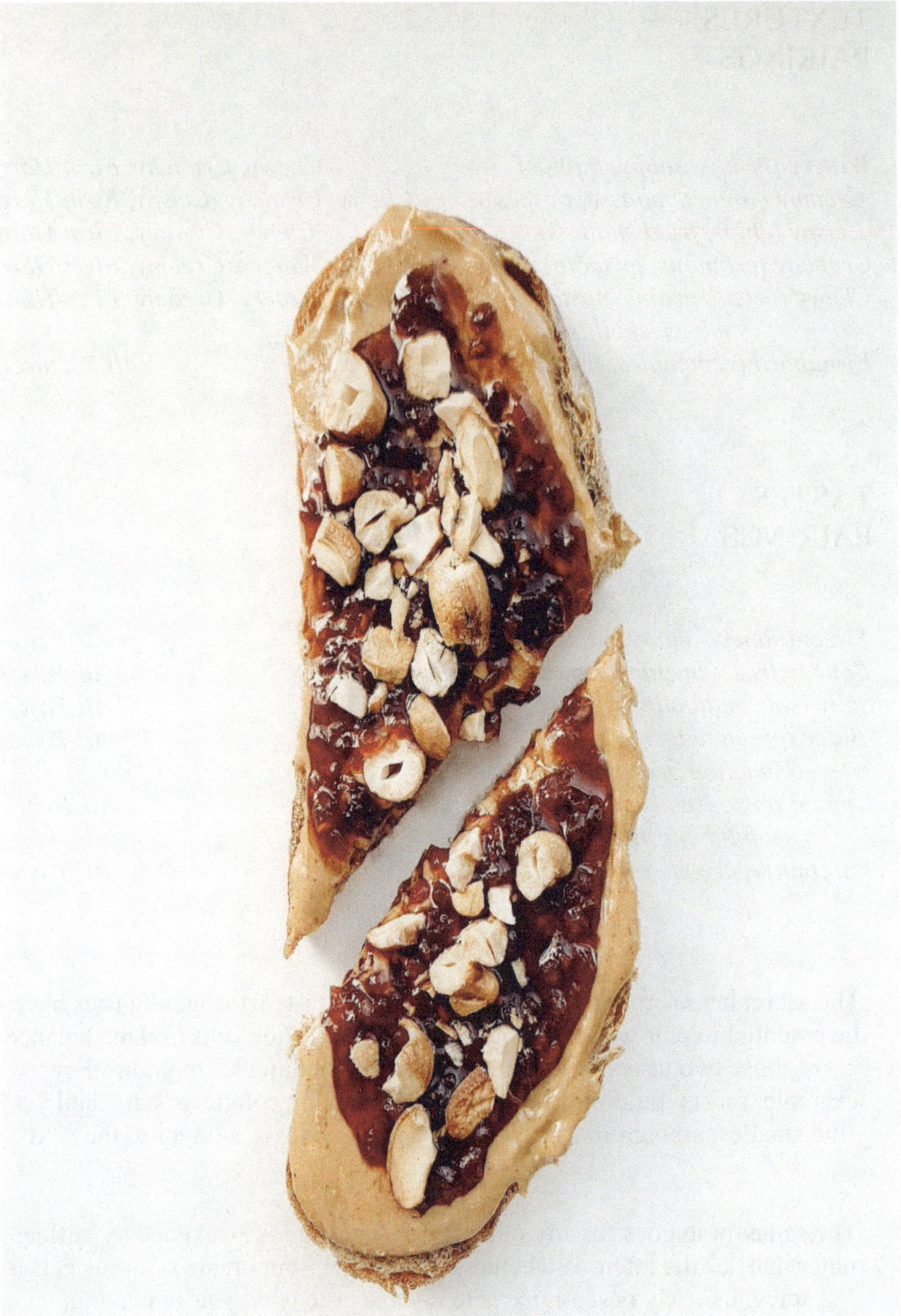

CASE STUDY

(Pictured: open-faced peanut butter and jelly with roasted peanuts). Peanut butter and jelly -- One of the most famous flavor combinations, like, ever. And for good reason! To break it down, PB & J works so perfectly because its taste is balanced; the fat in the peanut butter is contrasted by the sweetness of a jam or jelly. The chewy texture of the bread pairs best with the creamy textures of peanut butter and a fruit spread. If I were to put a spin on the traditional sandwich, I'd do it open faced as pictured, on a piece of toast and topped with a garnish of roasted chopped peanuts. Toasting the bread adds a crispy texture on top of the chewy, giving it more depth of mouthfeel. The same can be said for chopped peanuts, which not only look appealing as a garnish, but are functional and add a crunch that makes it more fun to eat. The smokiness of a roasted or toasted food also adds an appetizing aroma that adds to the whole experience.

PLATING YOUR DISH

Plating is where your personality gets to shine. In partnership with your flavors, it is what defines you as a creator and chef; it is your signature. Don't be afraid to try new things and play with different techniques and styles.

PLATING OBJECTIVES

1. Create dimension
2. Show off the main ingredient
3. Contrast textures and colors
4. Balance food portions
5. Select the right plate
6. Keep your garnishing simple

Creating Dimension & Contrast

I like to begin my plating by creating or looking at a sketch of how I want to serve my dish. It gives me a basic framework to go off of as I arrange foods on my plate. From there, I work to create height and balance to really give the dish dimension. Focus on creating both negative (empty) and positive (filled) space on the plate. This will not only give the presentation contrast but also shows your personal touch and style.

Balancing Food Portions

One of the most important things to consider in plating is portion size. Not only is this a consideration for visual appeal, but it is also one for the palate. If you've created a very flavorful dish, you want to prevent palate fatigue. To do this, you'll have to be thoughtful about how much of each component you serve on the plate. For example, if you're using something very salty like capers to garnish, use them sparingly so you don't overwhelm the dish with salt. You can always add more later if you think it needs it!

Picking the Perfect Plate

Picking the perfect plate takes a few considerations. The first is to choose a plate that matches the shape of your food; for example, a round plate is suitable for pancakes and a square plate for a brownie square. The second is to choose a color and style that will let your dish shine; white is always a great choice but a darker color like black could add greater contrast if the food is a lighter color.

The next to consider is the size of the plate itself. Think of the quantities you'll be using and choose a plate that won't make the food look too crowded or too sparse. Trust your gut on this one!

Plating

When arranging food, think of the plate as a clock. Place the protein between three and nine o'clock, the starches or grains between nine and twelve, and the vegetables between twelve and three. You can play around with portions and placement, but these rules are a good foundation for creating a beautiful plate that always pleases the eye.

Garnishing

You'll have to rely on your creative instincts to work your garnish and sauces into the dish, but make sure they're visible and complement the other elements. Most importantly, allow the food to show for itself and finish it off with a meaningful garnish. The best garnishes impact a dish through texture, flavor, aroma, and visuals. This is your chance to add your last personal touch and really make the dish yours. Remember, you eat with your eyes first.

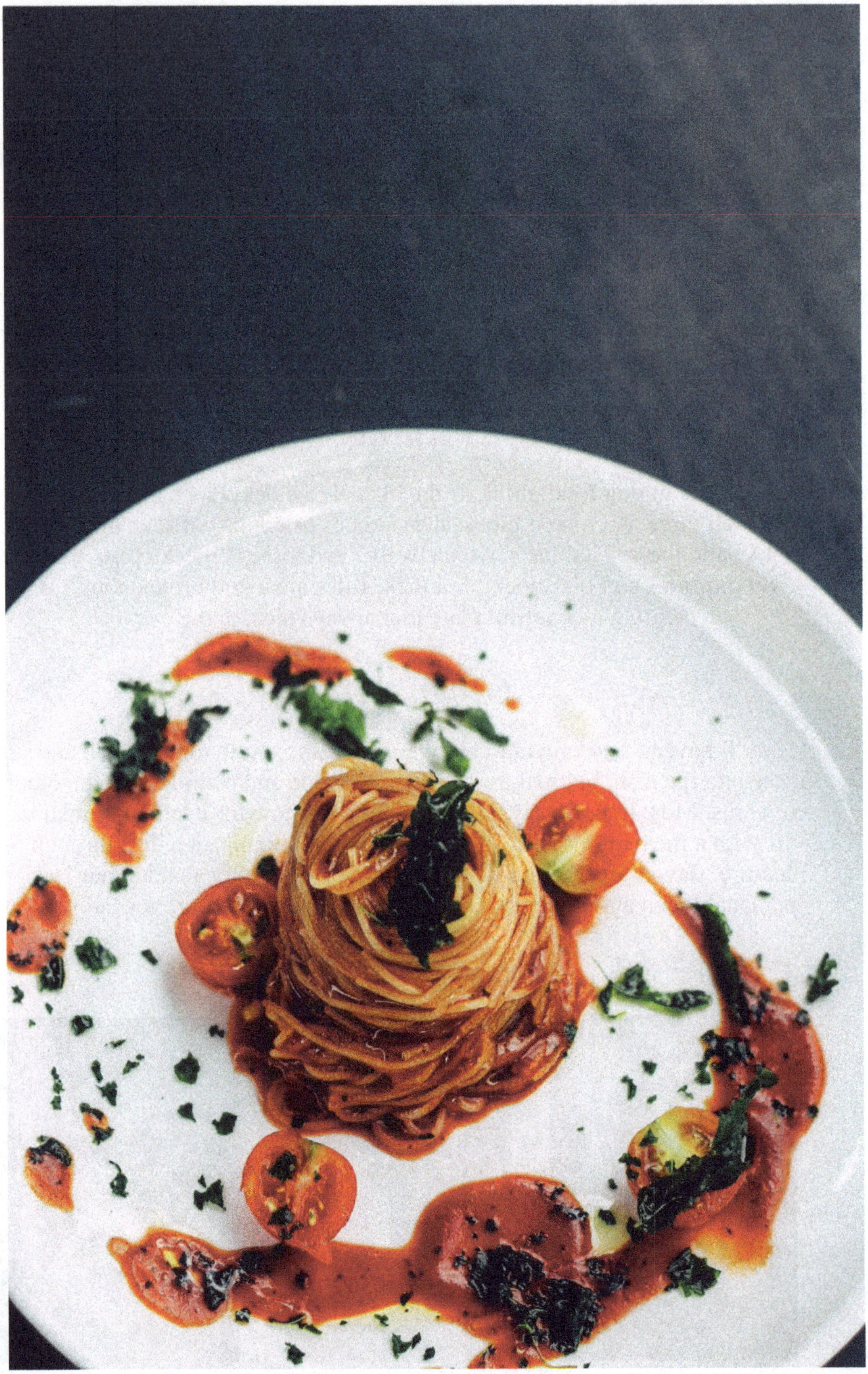

CASE STUDY

(Pictured: pasta with red sauce, lightly toasted basil, and sliced cherry tomatoes). Pasta is the comfort food we all know and love, and it's easy to elevate into a stunning plate that looks like more than the dinner you made in a pinch. The classic favorite is a large round white plate, the perfect canvas for a bright sauce and garnish with a swirl of pasta. There are countless choices for pasta varieties and sauces that can make interesting combinations and plating concepts. The garnish of a red sauce, sautéed greens, and fresh sliced tomatoes complement the flavor of the pasta and build dimension on the plate. To create a nest of pasta like this you can use a pair of tongs or a fork and spoon to twirl and place it onto the plate. Thinner varieties like angel hair or spaghetti are easier to arrange on the plate since they stick to each other nicely.

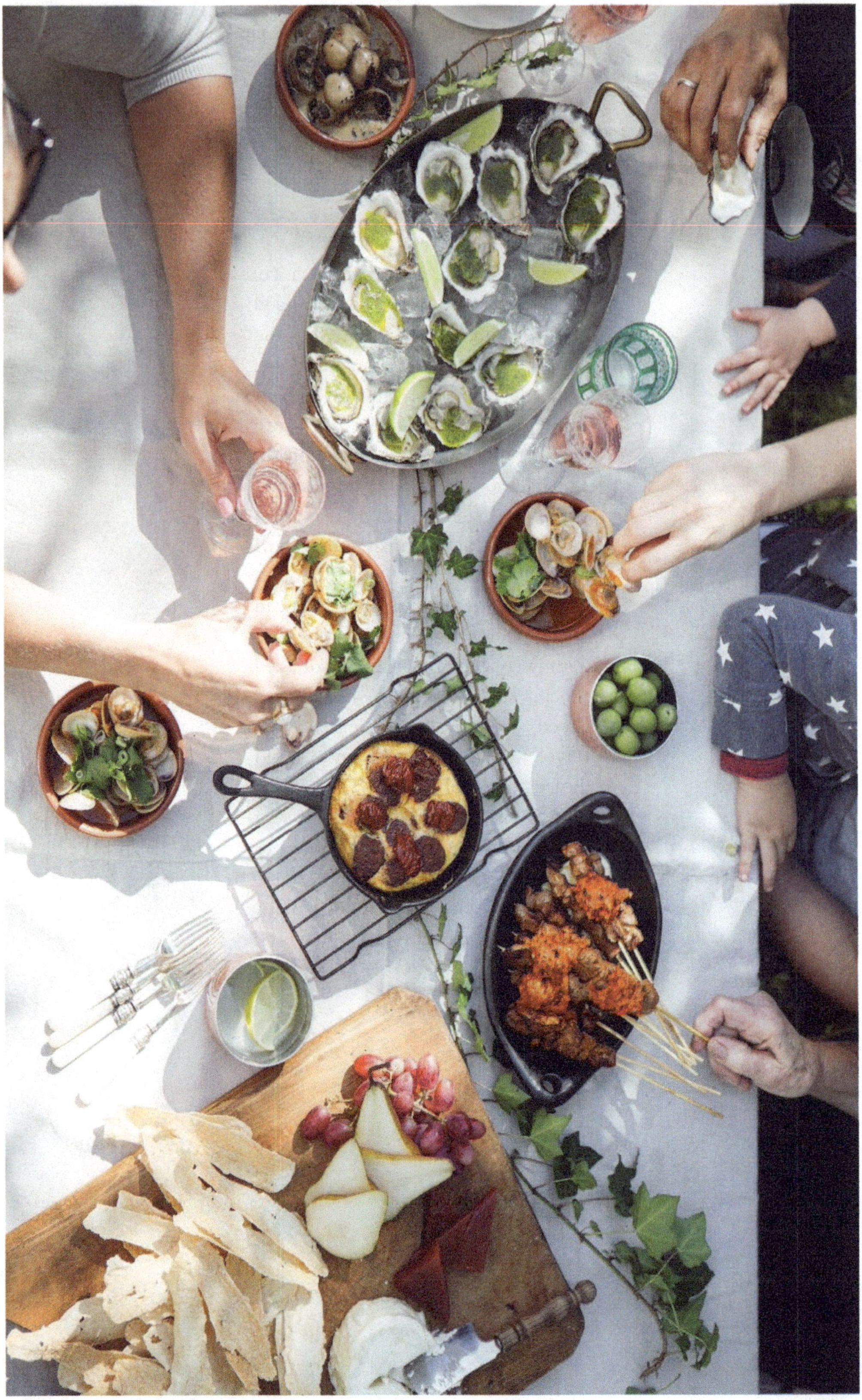

CULTIVATING AN EXPERIENCE

Garnishing is as much about what's on the plate as it is about what isn't. There are many other areas to engage with to create a dish and a moment that everybody will remember.

People are attracted to abundance.

Just think of the last time you went to a buffet or attended a holiday feast and felt the excitement of having so many options to choose from. It's enticing, and that's what makes it a great strategy to deploy at your next gathering, big or small.

Do what you can to create visual variety and options for your guests. Use tasteful plateware that pops off the table, make a centerpiece, light candles, lay out food in different sized and shaped dishes, set the table with napkins and silverware, and whatever else makes you happy.

Add layers to the dining experience. Think about serving multiple courses or create a special appetizer like a breadbasket to pass around the table before the main course. For drinks, try keeping them in pitchers and allowing guests to serve themselves. The pitchers will add an element of abundance and always look great on a table spread.

Consider the type of dining experience you'd like to have. Are you looking for something casual like a picnic or something more elaborate? From there you can decide the type of decorations and serving items you'll want, and then the kinds of foods and drinks you'd like to have. Your plan will begin to unfold once you know the direction you would like to take.

Make it fun. Pretty tablecloths, music, candles, decorations, flowers, you know the drill. You could make a special playlist or your own menu that lists the meals you'll serve. You could draw up place cards with guests' names on them or create an element of fun by asking people to dress up. To take things to the next level, you can buy a special bottle of wine or come up with a signature drink to serve with your dish.

I think that all food tastes better with good company. When you're putting a lot of effort into setting up a fantastic dinner or working hard on a culinary masterpiece, it feels even better to be surrounded by people who make you feel good. For me, garnishing has always been a reason to create something magical, but it always feels ten times better when you can share it with someone else.

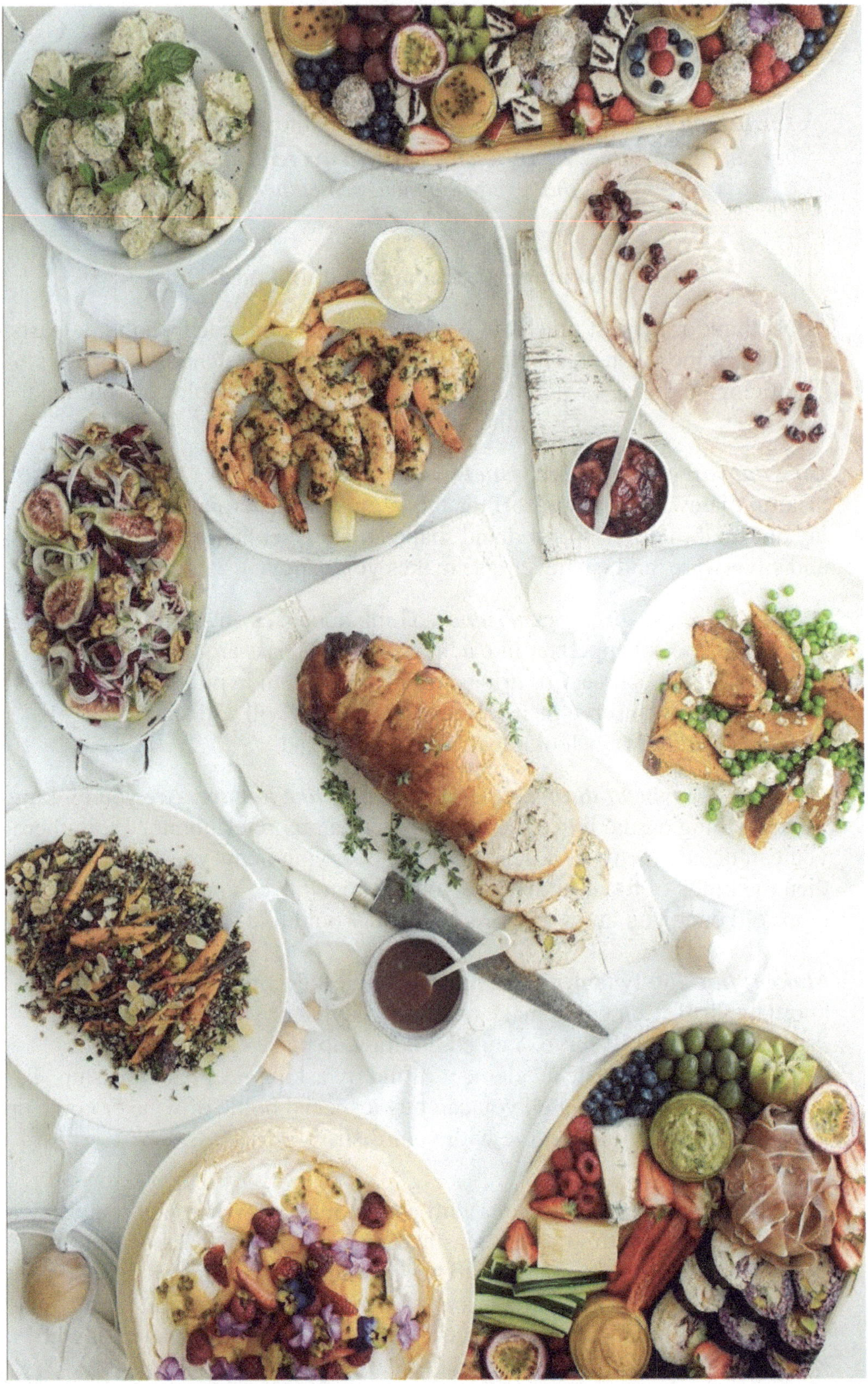

CASE STUDY

(Pictured: feast table with grilled shrimp, turkey, stuffed pork tenderloin, mixed fruit cake, roasted carrot couscous, fig and cabbage slaw, sweet potatoes, potato salad, and a charcuterie board). I think there is something so special about serving at the table. It can be fun to garnish big plates of food, especially if you're not in the mood to put heaps of attention into each individual serving. I've found that a lot of my friends and family really just enjoy serving themselves and being surrounded by lots of food and interacting with each other by passing plates along. That interaction is really part of the bonding experience of being at the table and sharing memories and stories too. Not to mention it's much easier to keep food hot and fresh, since you'll be serving it as a whole portion.

SIMPLE RECIPES

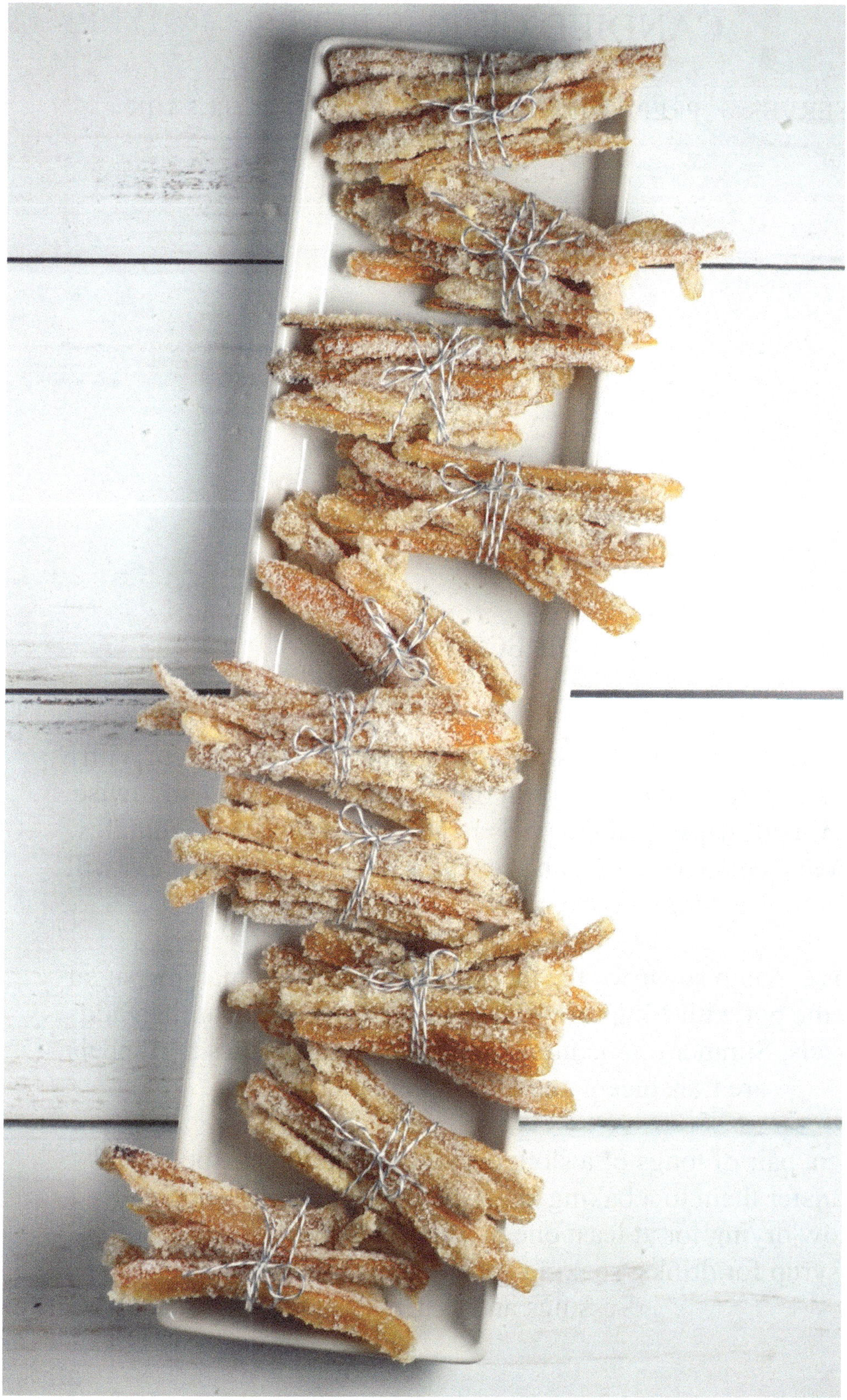

CANDIED CITRUS PEELS

SERVES: 6 | PREP TIME: 20 MIN | TOTAL TIME: 1 HR 5 MIN

INGREDIENTS

1 grapefruit
3 oranges
2 lemons
2 limes
1 ½ cups sugar
1 tsp vanilla

DIRECTIONS

Slice the ends of the fruits off and cut the peels from them with your knife. Keep the white pith on the peels and slice lengthwise into ¼ inch strips. Boil the peels in a pot of water for 15 minutes. Drain in a colander, rinse, and repeat. This blanching process will remove the bitterness of the peels.

Reserve ¼ cup sugar for the last step and add the remaining sugar into the pot with 1 cup of water. Boil to dissolve sugar then add the peels. Simmer on medium-low heat for 45 minutes until peels are translucent and a light syrup has formed.

Use a pair of tongs or a slotted spoon to remove the peels and transfer them to a baking sheet covered in parchment paper. Allow drying for at least one hour and up to one day. Save the syrup for drinks, soaking sponge cakes, or making salad dressings and marinades.

Use the remaining ¼ cup of granulated sugar to toss and coat the peels evenly. The peels can be kept for a month at room temp, and for months if kept in the fridge or freezer.

Candied peels can be eaten on their own or put into other recipes like stollen bread or panettone.

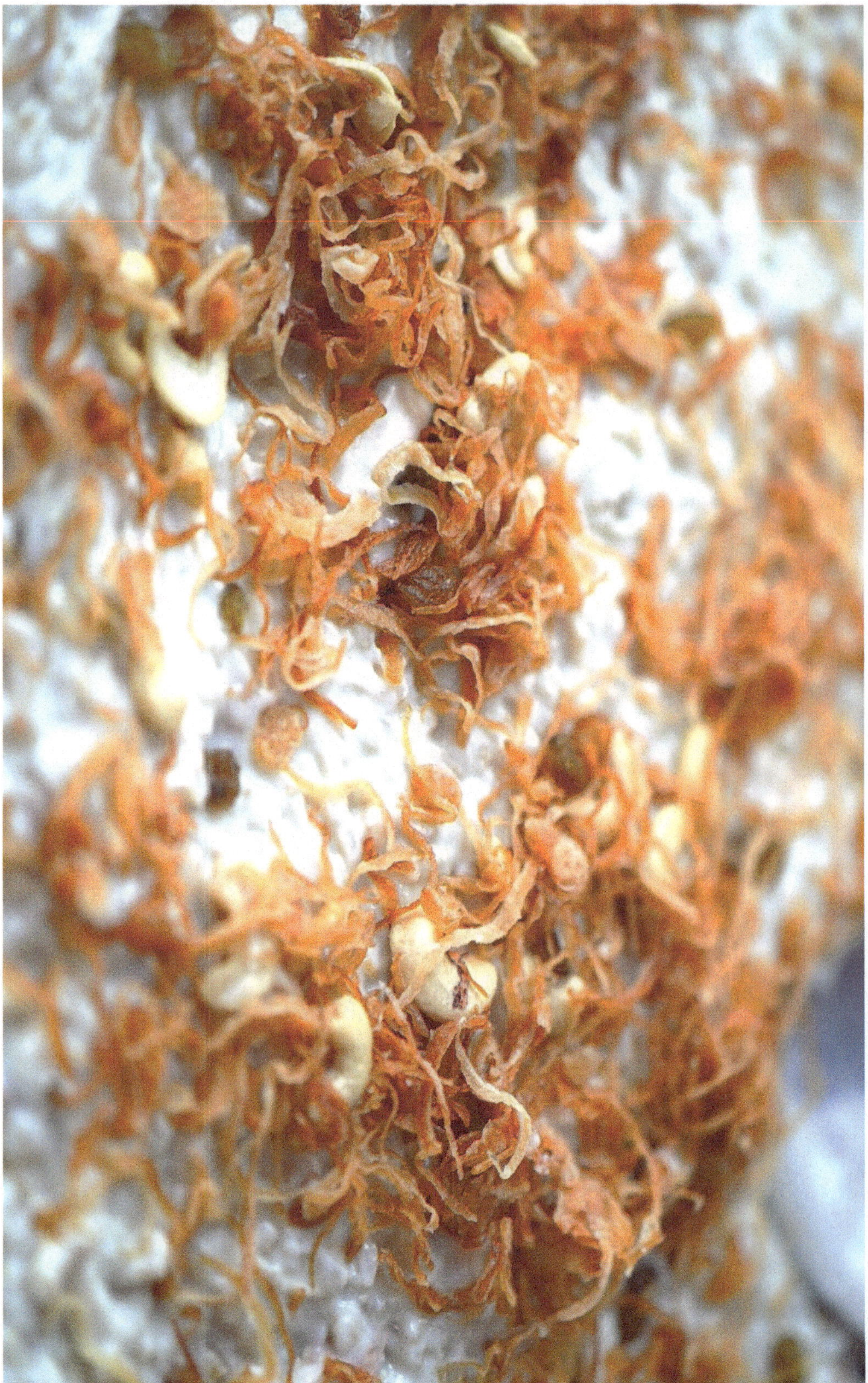

FRIED SHALLOTS

MAKES: ½ CUP | PREP TIME: 5 MINUTES | TOTAL TIME: 20 MINUTES

INGREDIENTS

4 shallots
1 cup vegetable oil
Salt

DIRECTIONS

Prepare a baking sheet with a layer of paper towels or a kitchen towel. This will absorb the fried shallot oil later on to keep them from getting soggy.

Peel and slice the shallots 1/8 of an inch thick or use a mandoline to get precise slices.

In a saucepan, add the oil and shallots to a small saucepan and put the burner on medium heat. Stir occasionally for 10-15 minutes, turn down the heat if oil begins to spatter.

The second they become golden brown, remove immediately using a sieve strainer and place onto your prepared baking sheet.

Dab gently to remove excess oil and allow to cool for 15 minutes. It's best to use them right away but you can store them in an airtight container for a few weeks too.

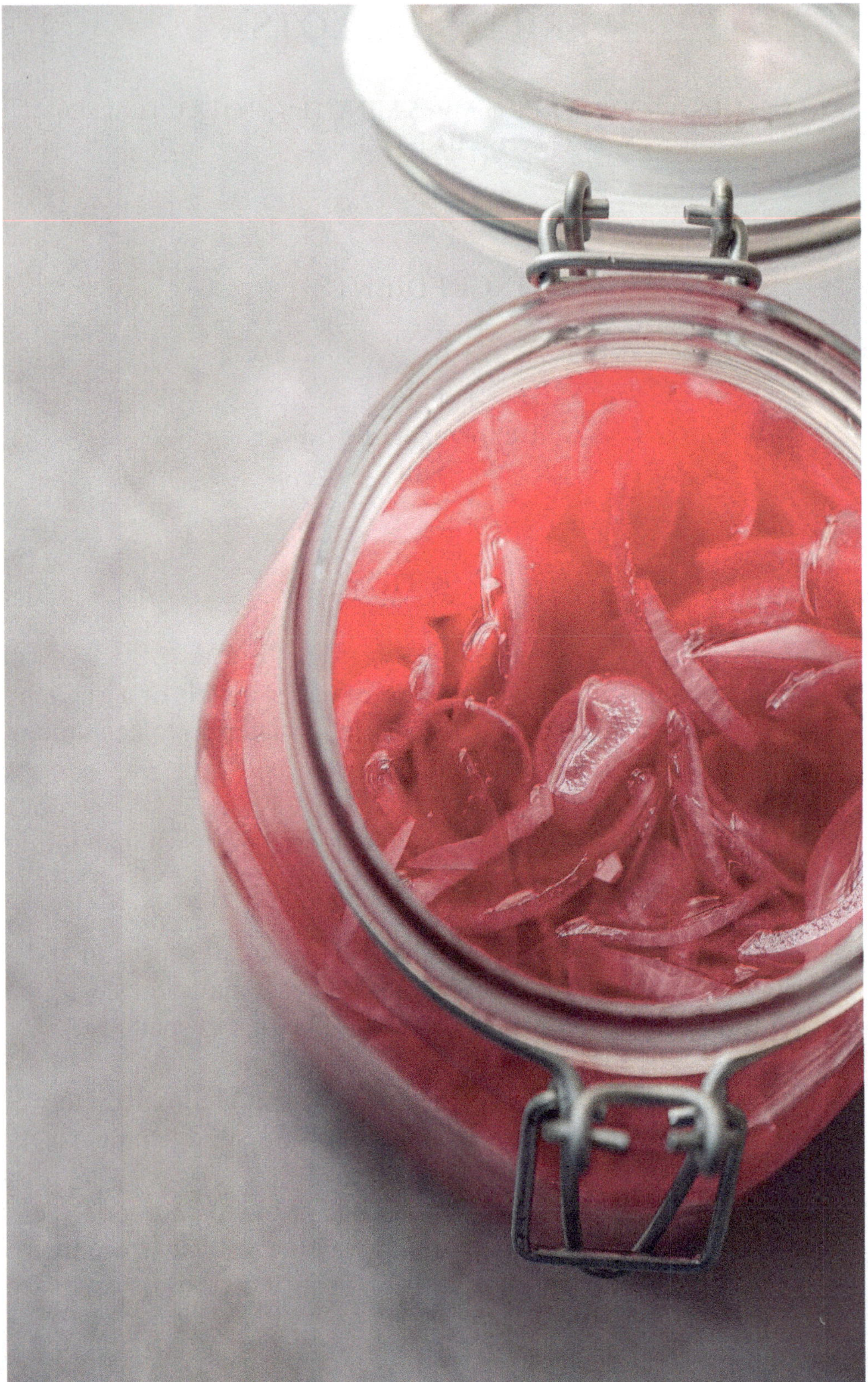

PICKLED ONIONS

MAKES: 1 PINT | PREP TIME: 5 MINUTES | TOTAL TIME: 10 MINUTES

INGREDIENTS

1 medium red onion
½ cup water
¼ cup apple cider vinegar
¼ cup white or red wine vinegar
2 tbsp honey
1 tsp sea salt
1/8 tsp ground black pepper (optional)
1 bay leaf (optional)

DIRECTIONS

Slice onion as thinly as you can, 1/8 inch or less preferably. Place in a mason jar or other heat-tolerant container.

Combine vinegars, water, and spices into a small saucepan and bring to a simmer. Allow it to bubble for 5 minutes.

Immediately pour over the jarred onions and seal with a lid. Allow cooling for a half hour. You can serve them or keep them in the fridge to continue pickling. They can be kept for 3 weeks in the refrigerator.

The brine can be reused to pickle other things or be worked into marinades or vinaigrettes.

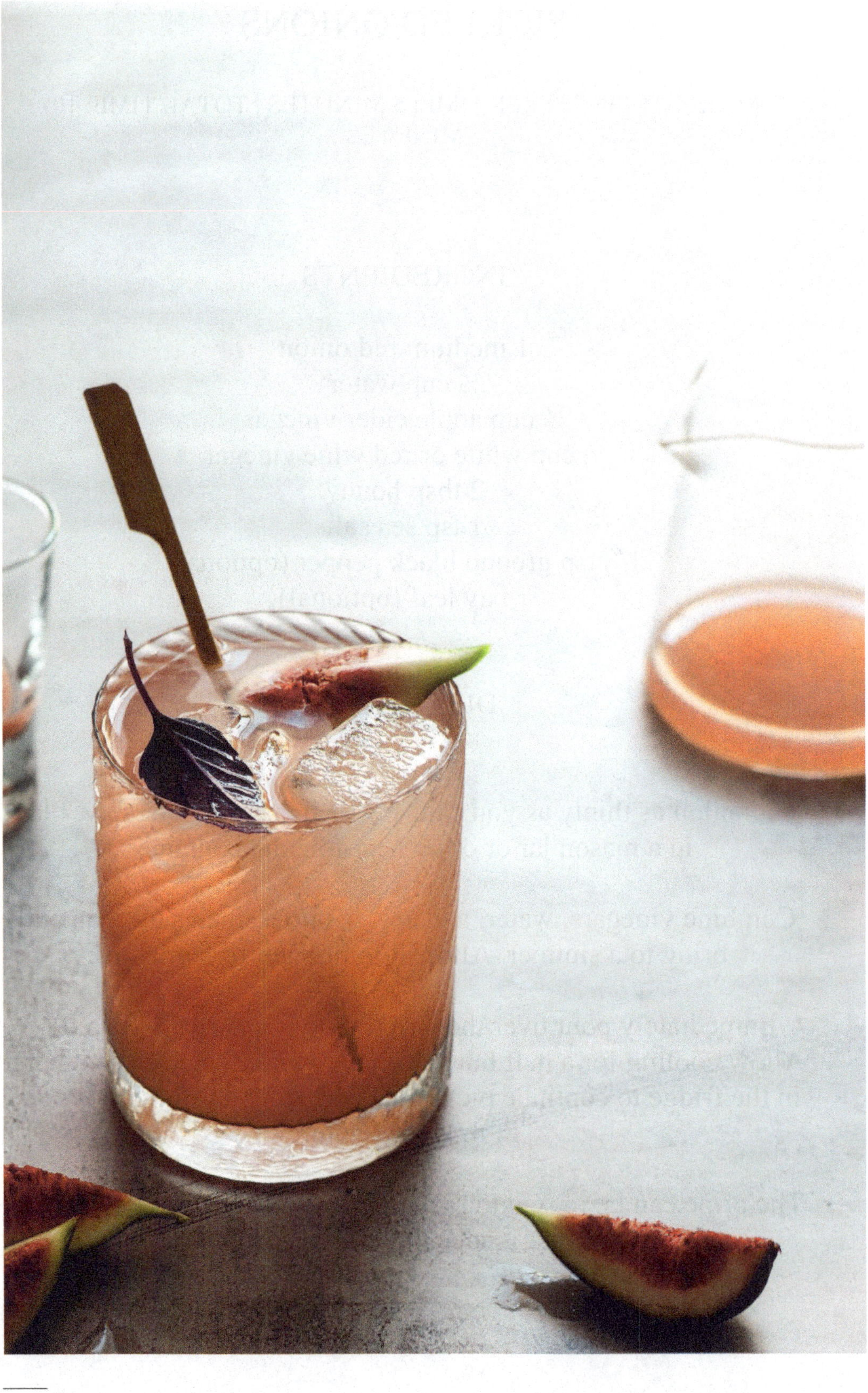

SIMPLE SYRUP INFUSION

MAKES: ABOUT ¾ CUP | TOTAL TIME: 40 MINUTES

INGREDIENTS

1 cup of granulated sugar
1 cup water
1 tbsp alcohol of choice (optional, lengthens shelf-life)

FLAVORS TO TRY

1 tbsp whole spices
4 tbsp chopped herbs
1 cup chopped fruit
¼ cup juice

DIRECTIONS

Combine sugar and water into a small saucepan. Stir until dissolved and bring to a boil.

Add your ingredient of choice and boil for 2 minutes.

Turn off the burner and allow the mixture to steep until cool (about 30 minutes).

Pour the mixture through a mesh sieve and into a sealable bottle, jar, or airtight container. Keep in the fridge for up to a month.

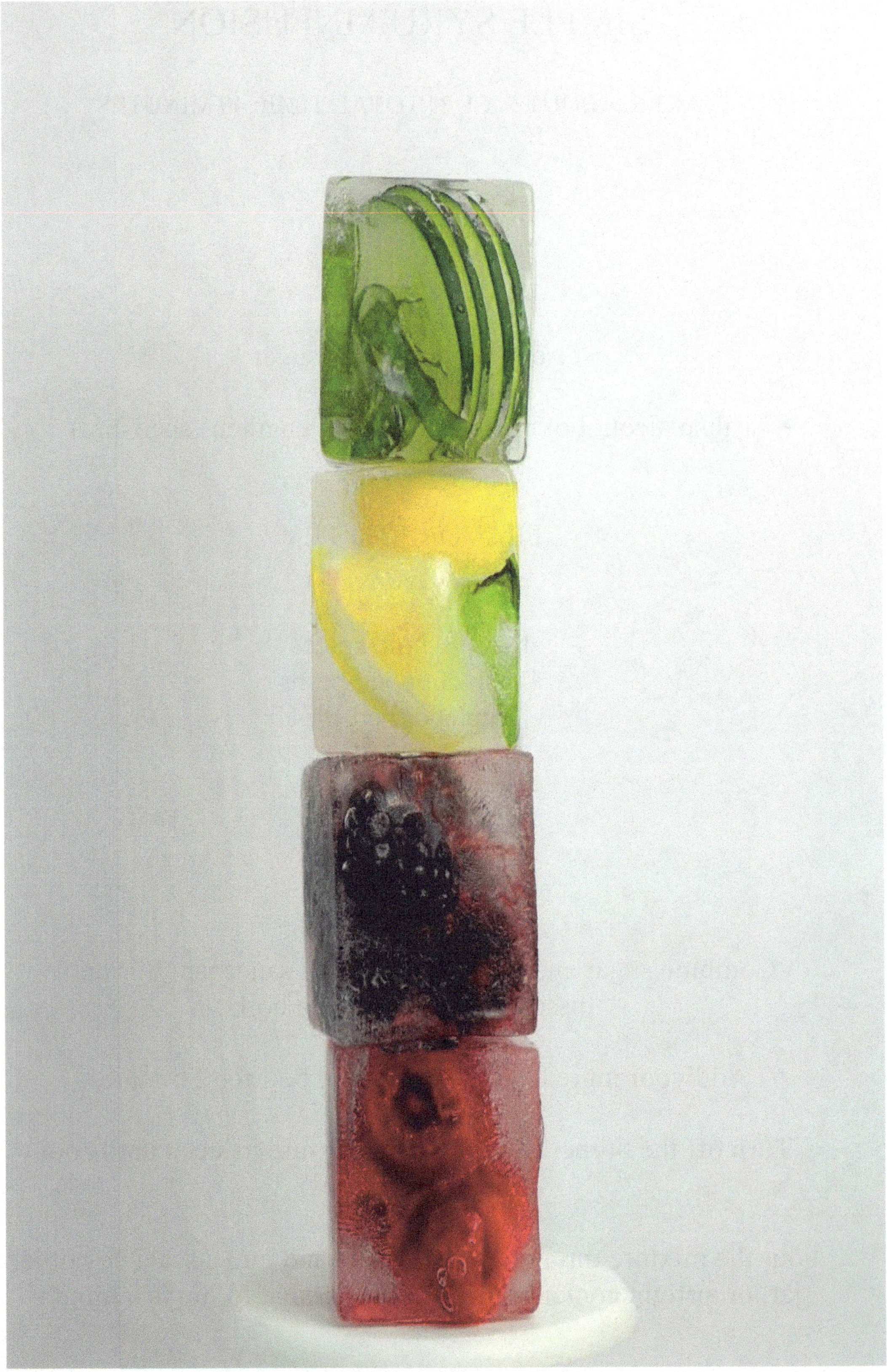

INFUSED ICE CUBES

MAKES: 1 TRAY | PREP TIME: 5 MINUTES | TOTAL TIME: 2 HOURS

INGREDIENT IDEAS

Crystallized petals
Infused syrups
Berries
Herbs
Tropical fruits
Juices
Purees
Coconut water
Coffee & Tea
Milk & Cream
Food grade essential oils

DIRECTIONS

In each cube of the ice tray place 1-2 pieces of fruit or herb leaves. Fill each cube with water or other liquid of choice. Place the tray in the freezer and let it rest for 2 hours.

TIPS

If using fresh herbs, bruise slightly to release the oils which will flavor the cubes.

Once the cubes have been frozen, you can pop them out of the mold and store them in a freezer-safe bag in the freezer for future use.

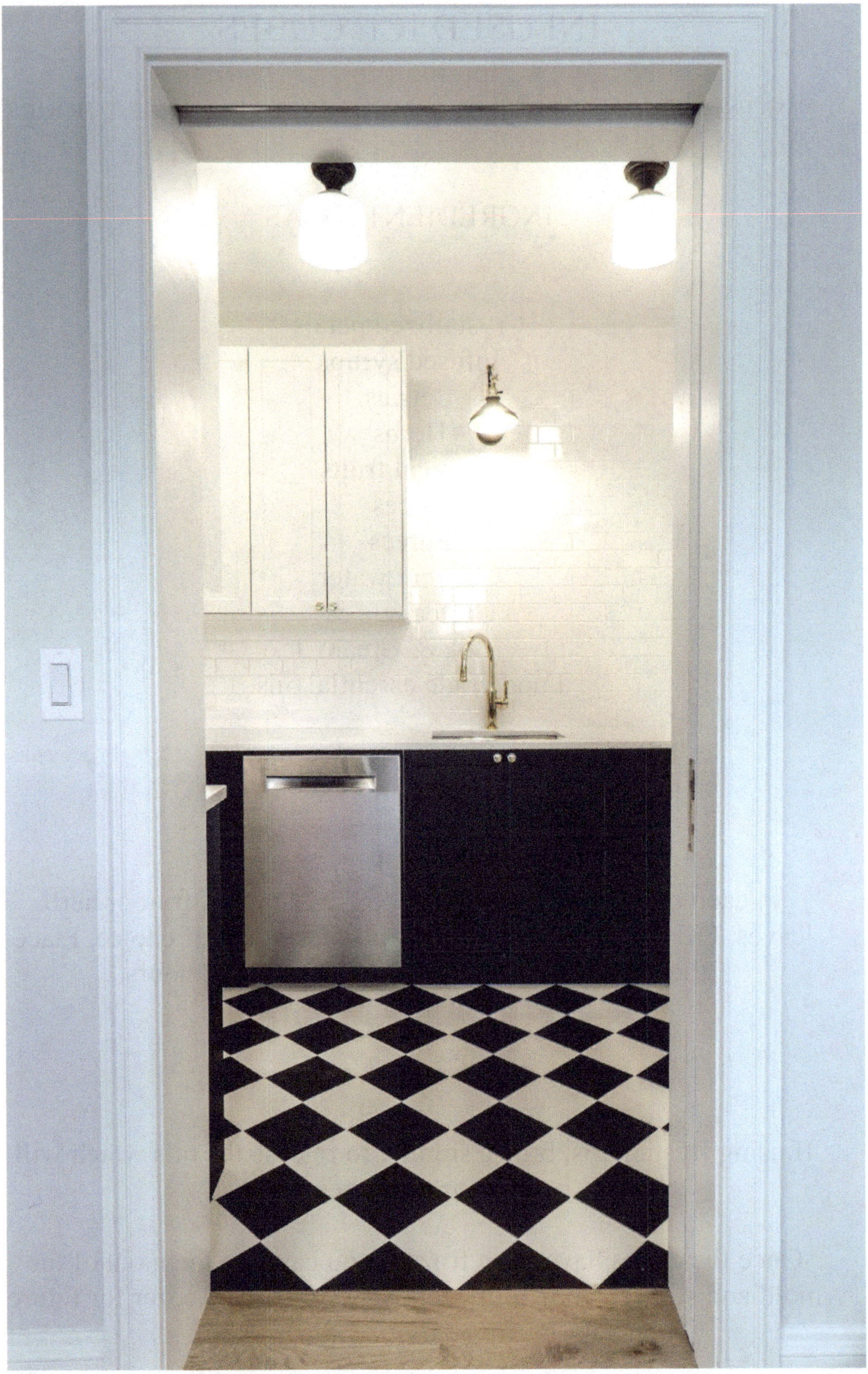

CONCLUSION

At its essence, garnishing is the art of doing more with less. When I began writing this book, I worried that I was spending too much time talking about flavors and plating because I wanted the focus to be on garnishing. I also realized that if I wanted to make a truly honest garnishing book, I couldn't leave out the other components of creating a great dish. Garnishing is the ribbon that ties the whole dish together, but it cannot make up for a bland package.

I'm a big believer in quality over quantity. I think that the secret to making something beautiful is accentuating what's already there and making it shine. By nature, a fantastic garnish shouldn't be complicated; it should be simple but executed with taste and attention.

That's really all that anything requires to thrive -- just some time and thoughtful attentiveness. If you practice and apply your creativity, you'll make tasteful garnishes and incredible food. In a frozen-food-fast-paced world, it can feel really difficult to connect with cooking, let alone making it look visually appealing.

I'm not a professional chef and I've never gone to cooking school, but there is something so simple and gratifying in being a home chef. Sometimes you'll cook for a whole table and other times it's just you in the kitchen wearing your pajamas, whipping up something that leaves you smiling because it's
just. that. good.

Garnishing is presentation. It's cooking. It's flavors. It's taste. It's aroma. It's chemistry. It can sound overwhelming and challenging, but it doesn't have to be. It's that last finesse you place on the plate, that one final puzzle piece -- your signature. It's you. And you deserve good food, amazing food, beautifully plated food that you can't wait to photograph and show to your friends.

I wrote *Garnish* with the intention that you would be able to follow along easily, be inspired to garnish your food, and not spend two weeks trying to figure out how to do it. I value your time and I truly believe that life is meant to be enjoyed. Food is an essential part of our every day, and it connects us in more ways than one. If we can find joy in those in-between moments -- in the taste-testing, the plating, and the garnishing -- life can be so much sweeter.

NOTES

There is an incredible abundance of information and talent available at our fingertips and it has made this book all the richer. I am so thankful for the many gifted and knowledgeable people who brought this book to life.

I would like to give special thanks to the very numerous and talented creators from Unsplash.com; they are the geniuses behind the stunning photographs woven throughout *Garnish*. Their names have been listed on the PHOTOGRAPHERS page in the order they appear in this book.

Of course, where would this book be if my boyfriend hadn't convinced me to write it? It would probably still look a lot like that messy sketch from "THE VISION" section and would most definitely be stained with coffee and stuffed inside of a notebook, never to be seen again. Thank you for your bottomless support and care packages, they have sustained me during my time as a desk rat.

Thank you to my wonderful family and friends, who have stuck with me throughout the writing of this book and have been the dependable taste-testers of my cooking career; your dysfunctional garnishes were the inspiration for this book. On behalf of all who will make better garnishes because of it, I thank you.

Lastly, I'd like to say a big thank you to my incredible editor, Melia Lenkner. Your advice, humor, and hard work made this process fun and exciting, just as it should be. I'm looking forward to the next book we work on together!

The last thank you is for you. I hope you enjoyed reading *Garnish* as much as I enjoyed writing it! On behalf of the nosh publishing team, if you'd like to share your garnishing creations with us we'd love to see them! You can send us a message through our website at noshpublishing.com or find us on Instagram @noshpublishing.

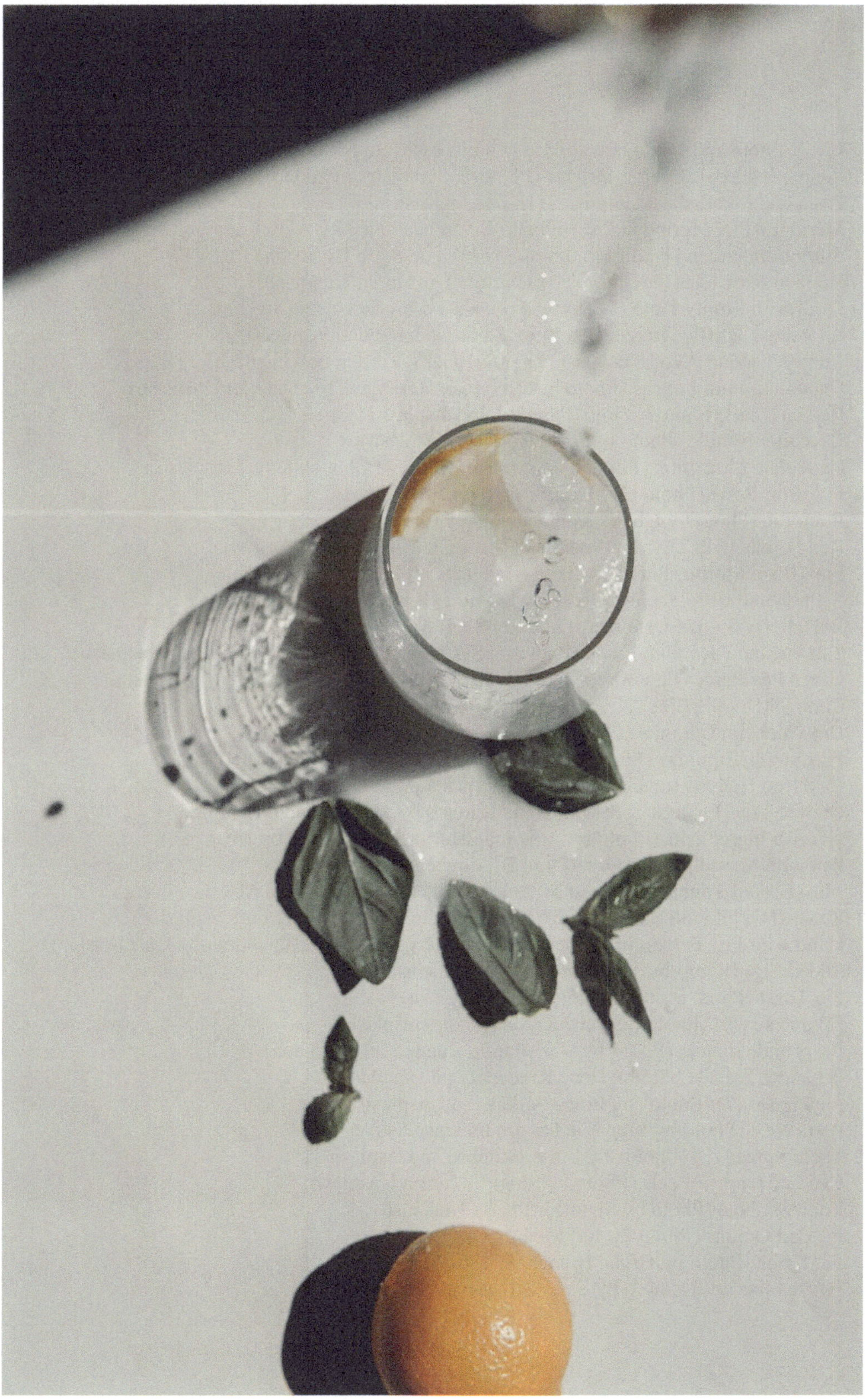

PHOTOGRAPHERS

Cover Photo and Lemons with Bag (Photos by Mathilde Langevin on Unsplash)
Poppyseed Loaf, Loaf & Drizzle (Photos by Gaby Yerden on Unsplash)
Pasta and Meatballs (Photo by STIL on Unsplash)
Meringue Pie, Meringue Pie with Blow Torch (Photos by Alex Loup on Unsplash)
Sifter with Green Handle (Photo by Erin Waynick on Unsplash)
Kitchen with Tiles (2) (Photos by Chastity Cortijo on Unsplash)
Stool with Empty Plate (Photo by s-o-c-i-a-l-c-u-t on Unsplash)
Chocolate Truffle Drizzle (Photo by Zahir Namane on Unsplash)
Cherry Tomato Avocado Toast (Photo by Gaby Yerden on Unsplash)
Chocolate Mint Leaves (Photo by American Heritage Chocolate on Unsplash)
Roe on Toast (Photo by Jojo Sharemy on Unsplash)
Lavender Bundle (Photo by rocknwool on Unsplash)
Chocolate Medallion (Photo by American Heritage Chocolate on Unsplash)
Plums in Bowl (Photo by Maria Siriano on Unsplash)
Plum Pie (Photo by Uliana Kopanytsia on Unsplash)
Red Drinks with Thyme (Photo by Rirri on Unsplash)
Pink Basil Mojito (Photo by Irene Kredenets on Unsplash)
Salmon and Citrus Foam (Photo by Edward Howell on Unsplash)
Blackberry Swirl Meringue (Photo by Sheri Silver on Unsplash)
Salmon and Rice with Purée (Photo by Sebastian Coman Photography on Unsplash)
Green Pea Purée (Photo by Vladimir-Gladkov on Unsplash)
Caramel Drizzle (Photo by Yulia Khlebnikova on Unsplash)
Brownie with Caramel (Photo by Priscilla Dupreez on Unsplash)
Pizza with Toppings (Photo by Pinar Kucuk on Unsplash)
Cast Iron Huevos Rancheros (Photo by Ijaaba A on Unsplash)
Orange Tree, Orange Tree with Hand (Photos by Jared Subia on Unsplash)
Garnish Ingredients (Photo by American Heritage Chocolate on Unsplash)
Pan with Mussels (Photo by Margo Brodowicz on Unsplash)
Mussels and Tomatoes (Photo by Anastasiia Rusaeva on Unsplash)
Roasted Quail with Saffron Rice (Photo by Vladimir-Gladkov on Unsplash)
Hand with Fig, Person in White Shirt (Photo by Anastasiia Balandina on Unsplash)
Sliced Figs (Photo by Tina Van Hove on Unsplash)
Fig Toast (Photo by Andreea Popa on Unsplash)
PB and J swirl (Photo by Irene Kredenets on Unsplash)
Pears and Granola (Photo by Christianne Koepke on Unsplash)
PB and J Toast (Photo by Irene Kredenets on Unsplash)
Pie Photos (3) (Photos by Praewthida K on Unsplash)
Pasta Nest (Photo by Mgg Vitchakorn on Unsplash)
Table Spread (2) (Photos by Luisa Brimble on Unsplash)
Candied Orange Peels (Photo by Sheri Silver on Unsplash)
Fried Shallots (Photo by Shameer PK on Unsplash)
Pickled Onions (Photo by Jeff Siepman on Unsplash)
Fig Drink (Photo by Bruna Branco on Unsplash)
Infused Icecubes (Photo by Sheri Silver on Unsplash)

ABOUT

PIA WARNER is an author, home chef, and professional creative. When she's not writing books for nosh, she's glued to her kitchen and powdered in flour.

NOSH BOOKS

This is **nosh**, a small independent publishing company dedicated to bringing you amazing content from unique sources. We're all about fitting big ideas into small packages (or books rather). Our works communicate information through engaging visuals paired with creative storytelling. We strive for **originality**, **aesthetics**, and **inspiration**.

As an independent publisher, we endeavor to offer you diverse content, collaborations, and voices from new writers and fresh topics.

The word nosh is derived from the Yiddish word "nashn", meaning to nibble or snack on. Just like a snack break, we want the works we produce to be part of your time to recharge. Our daily lives can be hectic and full of noise, craving something simple and satisfying. We created **nosh** with the intention to curate content just for these moments. Whatever your day brings, our wish is that you enjoy a nosh with us!

For more content, visit us at noshpublishing.com

nosh. *read & inspire*

Made in the USA
Las Vegas, NV
29 November 2023